KT-453-538

Joan B. Miller

The Casework Ministry

SCM PRESS LTD

334 00163 3

First published 1972
by SCM Press Ltd
56 Bloomsbury Street London

© *SCM Press Ltd 1972*

Printed in Great Britain by
Richard Clay (The Chaucer Press) Ltd
Bungay, Suffolk

scm centrebooks · christian casebooks

already published
Managing the Church / *W. E. Beveridge*
The Casework Ministry / *Joan B. Miller*

in preparation
Case Studies in Unity / *R. M. C. Jeffery*
The Christian in Education / *Colin Alves*
An Eye for an Ear / *Trevor Beeson*
Solitary Refinement / *Sister Madeleine* OSA

To W. H. B.
minister, pastor and teacher

Contents

Contents

Introduction

This book represents part of a Pilgrim's Progress. It is the outcome of a journey to find, not a way out of this world to a Celestial City but a way of living and working as a Christian in the twentieth century.

It is difficult to say where it began. Perhaps with a missionary grandfather who for some reason assumed that I would follow in his footsteps. He died when I was still a child and the memory remained as a kind of secret ambition, not to be a missionary but to be a minister. My mother's family had strong links with the local Methodist Church, where my maternal grandfather had been the first Sunday School Superintendent. I knew that women did not become ministers, but in the days before the Second World War the issue was a live one. Meanwhile I read French at Oxford and after obtaining my degree became a teacher and taught throughout the period of the war. In 1945 all my patient waiting seemed to be justified when the Methodist Conference accepted the principle of women in the ministry. In the following year however, after discussion by the Synods, it was decided to revoke the decision in such a way that the subject was not likely to be reviewed for the next twenty years.

I was shattered by this reversal and did not know what to do. I passionately desired to find some way to fulfil my sense of vocation, but no one to whom I turned for advice had much to offer in the way of help. One eminent minister attempted to persuade me to offer for the ministry of the Congregational Church which already accepted the principle of women in the ministry, and another told me categorically that I could not have a vocation to some thing that did not exist, and advised me to forget about it. In my days at Oxford Methodism had had very little influence on me. All my friends were Anglo-Catholics who had introduced me to the mystics. I thought of becoming a Catholic and entering a religious order. It was at this point that someone suggested that I wrote to the Warden of the Wesley Deaconess Order to explore the possibility of entering the order of women in my own church. I did so and after a lengthy correspondence with the Warden, the Rev. W. H. Beales, I entered the College at Ilkley to train as a Methodist deaconess. Of my year and a half at Ilkley I remember most of all the hours I spent in the Warden's study listening to W.H.B. and talking about Brunner and Barth, about the Catholic mystics and especially about the Quakers, Rufus Jones and Thomas Kelly. Above all I listened to a pastor talking about his ministry. Until that point my only church work had been preaching and I was an enthusiastic preacher. Now I learned about the pastoral ministry from a man who cared for people at depth and at cost. My desire for what Richard Jeffries called 'something greater that I knew' began to be transformed from a personal quest to a pilgrimage that could only be undertaken in relationship with other people.

For my month's vacation work I was sent to work in Coventry, and there encountered for the first time the problems of housing estates. The people begged me to stay with them and I jokingly wrote to the Warden and said that I was not coming back. He remembered this and when I had completed my training my first appointment was to a housing estate in Swindon. It was a tough assignment in which the stewards greeted me at my welcome meeting with the consoling remark, 'Nobody has ever done anything with X and no one ever will.'

It was during that time that I discovered the work of Charles de Foucauld and of the worker-priest movement. I felt immediately that their ideas about living out the Incarnation by being with people and not set apart from them was the only possible basis for my own ministry with people.

It was some years later on a housing estate in Basingstoke that I really began to see some of the ways of working out a ministry based on sharing the life of the people. For seven years I lived on the estate, and though for the first six years few people came to church I was overwhelmed by requests for help with social problems. I longed to help but had no idea where to begin and did not even know whom to contact for advice. Finally I felt I must have further training and asked for leave of absence to do some social studies and when this was granted, spent two years at Southampton University.

Here I discovered both sociology and casework. I realized then how much community studies would have helped me in my work on a housing estate. The casework theories answered my other great need: how to help people with a variety of problems when goodwill sometimes only results in making serious blunders. The training deepened my own self-awareness and heightened my sensitivity to other people's needs and reactions. I expected to go back to another housing estate, but the Deaconess Order was in need of a tutor to teach some social studies and I was asked to return to Ilkley. After a year of combining lecturing with pastoral care of a church I was allowed to do part-time social work with the teaching. There was a hospital in Ilkley which had no social worker and gladly accepted the hours of work I could offer. When the Deaconess College moved to Birmingham I remained as a full-time medical social worker.

During that time I learned a very different ministry from my former pastoral work, and yet I became increasingly convinced that at heart it was essentially the same. The gospel commission to serve people was present in everything I did. I was concerned with the biblical pursuits of housing the homeless (in welfare hostels or warden-supervised flats);

11

clothing the naked (with the help of the WRVS or social security grants); seeking the lost (usually long-lost wives, once a runaway daughter in the West Indies); defending the poor and helpless from officialdom, relatives or the gaps in the welfare state. Those five years were some of the richest and most satisfying of my life. With the team of nurses, doctors and hospital workers I was involved in a ministry that made me want to examine at depth the nature of ministry and how it may be accomplished today.

There were many people who by questions or dogmatic assertations spurred me on to make this study of ministry. There was the nurse, for instance, who asked me if I was any less religious now I was no longer employed in church work. There were those who asked why I should still continue in the Deaconess Order and be a social worker, and wanted to know what the difference is between me and an ordinary lay Christian social worker. There were also those who wanted an outline of the difference between a Christian and a non-Christian social worker.

The discussions of a group of working ministers who met twice yearly at William Temple College helped me to order my thoughts and encouraged me to try to express them. On the one hand I have found that many ministers are anxious to know something of the sort of training that social workers receive. They feel at a disadvantage in a helping situation, since people are used these days to receiving help from workers trained in personal relationships. I am now engaged in training social workers at Cardiff University, and we receive applications from clergy of all denominations for our courses in social training. Some of these have no intention of working in the statutory social services but see the training as an added and valuable tool for their ministry. Others wish to practise as social workers because they see this as a modern expression of ministry. There are also those, many of them young, who have a strong sense of vocation but do not feel able to accept the calling of the traditional ministry. It is for these three groups of people that I have written this book: for those wanting to know what casework is about; for those who may feel that a course of training could add value and insight to their ministry; and for those social workers who want to explore some of the meaning of their work.

1   What is Ministry?

To the man and woman in the pew the question 'What is Ministry?' would seem very simple. Candidates for a Deaconess Order, when asked why they wanted to give up a worthwhile job like teaching or nursing usually replied that they wanted 'to do full time service for God'. They never questioned their assumption that some work is service for God and some is not. In fact they accepted absolutely a definition of ministry that is based only on a part of the apostolic commission. The twelve were sent out to preach but also to heal the sick and cast out demons. In the apostolic succession the ministry has become preaching in the Protestant Church and the administration of the sacraments in the Catholic tradition. There has grown up the idea that this is real service for God, though other work may be done to his glory. Ministry, therefore, is done by the person who spends his time preaching, or in the many occupations that are in essence designed to bring people into the church to listen to the sermon. Both the men and the women who offer to the ministry and those to whom they minister accept this definition and question only whether it is done well or badly.

The gospels pose a different question and offer a different ideal. The gospel tradition has at the core two unmistakable principles, both of which are essential to real ministry; togetherness and wholeness. The first is the means by which the second, the goal of human existence, is achieved. Togetherness is summed up in the theological doctrine of the Incarnation and is therefore implicit in the whole of the New Testament. Without it there is no gospel and no salvation. It is extraordinary that the Christian church could ever lose sight of this doctrine, without which there would be nothing to preach, but since separateness is of the essence of original sin, it is a constant temptation, to which the church continually succumbs.

Looked at from this angle it appears that the current idea of ministry is based on apartheid, which is the antithesis of Incarnation. The very dress of the minister makes it clear at once that he is not to be confused with the common man, whether he is a religious in a monk's cowl and tunic or a parson in clerical grey and reversed collar. Once the monk's home-spun identified him with the people; now it only makes him appear an anachronism. The enclosed convent or monastery underlines the apartheid that pervades ministry today; it is only less obvious in the vicarage that is a country mansion or the house in the commuters' suburb of the minister who runs the down-town city mission. It is seen on every mission station where the missionaries live the lives of white settlers while 'ministering' to the natives.

From time to time the true nature of ministry has been demonstrated, usually in a rebellious movement. Such a passionate feeling of indentification inspired St Francis to leave his wealthy home and make common cause with the beggars and lepers. The urge towards togetherness did not long survive the founder. In the same way the original impulse that drove John Wesley out of his church to the crowds of illiterate, half-savage industrial workers and miners did not survive once he was dead, Methodism became a church and therefore joined the ranks of the respectable.

The most heroic evidence of the Incarnation since John Wesley has been the worker-priest movement in post-war France. The theology of ministry in its original gospel form was worked out in those few dramatic years in a way that is reminiscent of the very early days of the church when the faithful had all things in common. The movement began during the Nazi occupation of France, when great numbers of people were taken off to Germany to work there in factories. No chaplains were permitted to go with these workers and a group of priests obtained permission to volunteer as workers and travel to Germany incognito. This experience of living and working with the enforced conscripts was a revelation to these priests. They saw how they might come out of the ghetto of their parish church and share the life of the masses who had for so long been estranged from the church.

After the war a report on the state of religion in France was published with the title *France pays de Mission*. This was later translated into English and given the title *France Pagan?*[1] This report made it clear that France was a missionary country and that there was no point in priests continuing to conduct services in empty churches, for the people were so estranged from the church that there was no hope that they would return to an institution that had become completely foreign to them. Young priests responded enthusiastically to this challenge and were prepared to exchange the soutane for the workman's overalls, in order to be with the people who no longer wanted to be on church premises. Henri Perrin[2] was one of these. He had been to Germany and had discovered there a new vocation to be with men and not apart from them. He used the word 'ghetto' to describe the state of the church, not only of the clergy but also of the laity who have drawn apart into church movements and meetings, church newspapers and groups all dissociated from secular life.

Henri Perrin was a member of the Society of Jesus. When he returned from Germany he joined the worker-priests in the Mission de Paris. He worked there for three years, and after breaking off to serve his tertianship with the Society, he asked permission to leave the Jesuits as he felt that his vocation as a worker-priest could not be reconciled with the entire disposability required by the Society. He was accepted by the Archbishop of Sens as a worker-priest and allowed to join the work site at Notre Dame de Briancon, where the

17

Isere-Arc dam was being constructed. Soon after he arrived a strike broke out on the site. The conditions were dreadful; the men lived and worked as slaves and neither working nor living conditions were fit for human beings. Henri Perrin was elected to the strike committee and was soon acting as its secretary and issuing the daily communiqués. This strike resulted in a victory for the workers and considerable improvement in their conditions ensued. The peace did not last long. When a workman was killed, the thirteenth fatal accident on the site, Henri Perrin felt obliged at the funeral to say something about the responsibility of the management for the lack of safety precautions. Soon a list of dismissals was posted up, which included Perrin's name. The management could not be persuaded to reconsider its decision, so the men came out on strike. Finally the firm lost the case but by then interest had shifted from Isere-Arc strikes to the worker-priest movement.

In January 1954 the bishops sent a circular letter to the worker-priests under their jurisdiction, forbidding them to do full-time work or to belong to any organizations, or accept responsibility in any trade union. This meant the end of the worker-priest movement as it had been envisioned by its founders. Some of the priests submitted to the church; others felt they could not obey and waited in their jobs, hoping that the church might eventually relent. Henri Perrin was torn between his loyalty to the church and his vocation to the workers. He asked for time to think it over, certain only of one thing, that he could not go back to the ghetto. It is not possible to say what he would have done, as he kept silent about his struggles at this time and on 25 October 1954 he was killed on his motor-cycle on his way to work.

The worker-priest movement in France has been the cause of much discussion and controversy. No one can say with any certainty why Rome suddenly insisted that the priests should stop working. The reasons given were the spiritual dangers to the priests and the threat of communism, that it was claimed was influencing the priests more than they were evangelizing the proletariat. More cynical commentators saw in the decision the influence of big business interests threatening the church with the withdrawal of their support, if priests were allowed to back strikes and agitate for better working conditions as Henri Perrin had done. Certainly the withdrawal of the worker-priests did nothing to evangelize the masses and made life more comfortable for the management. Nothing in the history of the church since the Reformation had made such an impact on the people of France as this experiment. Its sudden ending was a disillusioning experience, not only for the people to whom the church seemed real and relevant for the first time but also for the priests, many of them young, who had found in the movement a ministry which challenged them to the fullest extent of their powers. The traditional mode of priesthood was so obviously ineffective in the face of the world of the twentieth century, that the missionary spirit of the worker-priest movement inevitably appealed to many priests, eager to find a way to minister to their generation.

In spite of repeated condemnation from Rome the worker-priest movement has had a profound influence on the thinking of the church about ministry. In England the established church has been most influenced by this movement. It has resulted in a number of very different experiments. On the one hand there are priests who follow the French pattern exactly and who work in industry as manual workers. These priests are all in their jobs with the knowledge and support of their bishops. There has been no attempt to publicize their work, but also no attempt to persecute them. Many people are unaware of their existence, and indeed some of the priests feel that they must remain quietly anonymous, pursuing what they feel is their vocation, but making no effort to advertise themselves as worker-priests. The Methodist Church, which has always prided itself on its links with the working class, remained untouched by the movement for some time in its offical policies but has now recognized the validity of ministries other than the traditional ones of preaching and pastoral work. Some individual ministers have been profoundly influenced by this revolution in ministry and have obtained official permission to serve as worker-ministers. The Baptist Church, in January 1970, proposed reducing the number of full-time ministers from 1,300 to 400 and training men to be part-time ministers, who would contrive to earn their living in industry. This is not unlike the Anglican scheme for a supporting ministry.

There have been other developments in England of experimental ministry. The best known of these is the Bishop of Southwark's scheme. This was a worker-priest plan in reverse: instead of ordained priests taking up secular employment, laymen have received theological training and have been ordained, while remaining in their ordinary jobs. These jobs are not necessarily manual labour or in a factory, as were the French worker-priests. The dean of the Southwark chapter is a master baker, who boasts he has never missed a a day's work in all the years in which he was undertaking his theological training. Others who have been trained under the Southwark scheme include a bank clerk, a bus conductor and civil servants. The scheme makes invalid the accusation that the church takes men from their natural environment and turns them into respectable middle-class professional workers, regardless of their origins. When David Wilson, the Kennington baker, said he was running the family business established in the last century and he was still living in the house in which he was born, another priest said regretfully that he had never returned to the place where he grew up, since he had trained to be a priest. The French worker-priests were concerned about this 'brain-washing' and alienation of theological students, that made them all come out in the accepted bourgeois mould. The Bishop of Southwark's scheme makes this impossible, for he trains a man in the place where he is and ordains him into the priesthood in the environment in which he is exercising his ministry.

There is a third group of worker-priests. They are a very varied group, mostly Anglicans but with a few nonconformists and one or two Roman Catholics. They include some of the second group and a few of the first, but in the main they differ from the original worker-priest movement in that they are not manual workers. The original small group encountered each other through correspondence in *New Christian*. They now meet twice yearly for conferences at William Temple College. There are three divisions in this group. The greater number of these priests are teachers, some in large comprehensive schools, some in colleges of further education and some in village schools. They are not solely concerned with religious instruction, though they may include it among subjects such as maths, liberal studies, architecture or any other subject in which they may be qualified. There is a tradition in the Anglican church of teaching being a job for the parson, so these men are not considered very unorthodox. Another group work in industry, but not on the factory floor. Some are personnel officers, others hold posts of responsibility for which they are qualified. The third group have undergone training in social work and work as probation officers, mental welfare officers or child-care officers.

These men prefer to call themselves working ministers to distinguish them from the worker-priest movement. The most striking difference is that whereas the original worker-priests deliberately chose to work in jobs that used less than their ability, these priests are for the most part doing work that uses all their gifts and education. They are as much a part of the working world, but their colleagues are not unskilled workers but their equals in every sense and they have to hold their own in this highly competitive society. They do not reject promotion when it comes, and some, for instance the social work group, have undergone specialized training in order to do their work.

Most of these men are married and have an ordinary family life. They vary in their attitude to the traditional parochial ministry. Some are attached to a parish in a part time capacity and help regularly by taking services at week-ends. They believe that this is vital to their ministry. Others have no such link and do not believe that this is essential. For them their work is their ministry and it is irrelevant to their priesthood to supplement it by preaching or other parochial duties. Most are concerned that the church should share in the insights that they are gaining in their working ministry, though some believe that the parish set-up has out-lived its usefulness and that the seeds of renewal are else-where. Some have a very high church attitude to their priest-hood, and others are wrestling to find a meaning in their ordination that will make it relevant in today's industrial society. This group is not structured and has no clear notion of its purpose except to explore the meaning of ministry in today's world. The link between the very different members is their concern to find a relevant ministry. Most are dis-satisfied with the present organization as it is seen in all the orthodox churches; none claims to have found the answer yet.

The last word has by no means been said about a working ministry. In November 1969 *The Guardian* reported that the Bishop of Riobamba in Equador had suggested the abolition of all thirty-eight parishes in his diocese and had recom-mended that the priests should go out and live and work with the people. The priests should support themselves by their earnings and should charge no fees and take no col-lections. Laymen should be trained, he suggested, until they were ready to be promoted to the status of deacon. The priests could then say mass and hear confessions and the deacons take over the other pastoral duties. The scheme must have been a surprise to Rome, after the condemnation of the much less revolutionary worker-priest movement in France. It is clear that there is a ferment in the church. Neither condemnation nor blank refusal to listen can silence the voice of the working ministers, who believe that the hard core of ministry depends neither on places nor clothes but that it is exercised wherever there are men and women to whom the Incarnation is a basic reality, and who are prepared to live out its implications.

NOTES

1. Maisie Ward, *France Pagan?*, Sheed & Ward 1949.
2. Henri Perrin, *Priest Workman in Germany*, Sheed & Ward 1949, and *Priest and Worker: Autobiography of Henri Perrin*, Macmillan 1965.

2 What is Casework?

In the search for forms of ministry that are relevant to today's needs there are a number of possible solutions and it is unlikely that one particular form will be all-sufficient. In fact the uniformity of the current pattern of ministry and its comparative inflexibility is one of its disadvantages. The urgent need is on the one hand for adventurous experiment in ministry, and on the other hand for thoughtful examination of a number of occupations to discover to what extent and in what ways they demonstrate aspects of ministry. Obvious examples are the long-established vocations of teaching and healing. Social work is a newcomer in the professions, but many who practise it are keenly aware of the vocational nature of their work. It therefore presents a legitimate subject for study as a valid sphere in which ministry may be exercised.

Social work in this country, like so many of our institutions, has a double origin: one in the voluntary work that culminated in the Charity Organization Society; and the other in the statutes of the Poor Law. The word casework, for instance, was used by the Charity Organization Society, though with a rather different meaning, but it has its roots in philanthropy. The child-care officer stems from the other source and fulfils many of the functions of the Poor Law guardian, arranging for boarding out or fostering, adoptions and the placement of children in institutions. The voluntary origins of social work are more often emphasized than the statutory, perhaps because of our national tendency to believe that good works are only really good if not done for money, as we suspect the motives of anyone who receives a reward for helping other people. The nineteenth century abounded in philanthropists, many of whom had a rooted dislike of the Poor Law since they believed that it turned the poor into paupers, robbing them of their independence by handing out benefits. The Charity Organization Society attempted to bring order into the chaos of private charity by systematic investigation of cases and by enlightened giving which would encourage the deserving poor to help themselves. The very thorough and exhaustive inquiry that their workers made before any decision was reached on a case was called the casework. The first training given to social workers was to teach them the theory and practice of these inquiries. Their attitude to those they helped, especially their division of the poor into the deserving and the undeserving, is not congenial to modern social workers who have different standards. Their insistence on the need for a thorough understanding of the circumstances if help is to be effective has been a good legacy.

Social work in this country continued to develop in two streams until the coming of the welfare state. On the one hand there were the Poor Law officers who were government workers, and on the other hand there were the social workers who had mostly arisen as the result of voluntary effort; the probation officers, the psychiatric social workers and the almoners. With the welfare state the Poor Law officers disappeared and their functions were divided among the welfare and mental health departments. The Curtis Report led to the Children's Act of 1948 which set up the children's departments and instituted a new kind of social worker, the child-care officer. Many of these new social workers were untrained, although courses in child care were set up to train as many as possible of the new workers with children. It was not until the Young-husband Report of 1957, however, that training courses were provided for welfare and mental health officers. These Certificate in Social Work courses held in colleges of further education and polytechnics were soon training a great variety of workers. The method of training for these workers is basically the same as that used on the courses already established in the universities. This method is called social casework.

Social casework in the modern sense came originally from American theory of social work and many of the basic textbooks on the subject are still American. Casework has become not merely a technique that can be taught but also a theory of life, so that it is to some extent a philosophy as well as a craft. The basis of both the theory and the practice is responsibility. The mandate of social work is the responsibility of the individual. Responsibility has two meanings in this context. It implies firstly a person's right to live his own life, to make his own decisions and, within certain limits of childhood or extreme illness of body or mind, to choose what he shall do with his life. Responsibility also implies man's ability to respond and so his capacity for growth and change. Casework rests on these twin concepts of self-determination and growth; man's right to be himself and man's endless potential for development.

This belief in man's capacity for development involves the formulation of theories as to how this can be achieved. Casework theory is based on the principle of relationship and the conviction that change can be effected in and through relationship with other people. Biestek, in *The Casework Relationship* says: 'It would be hard to exaggerate the importance of the relationship in casework, not only because it is essential to effective casework but also because it is the practical living out of our basic convictions about the value and dignity of the human person. It is based upon a philosophy of life which is both realistic and idealistic, which encompasses matter and spirit, reason and faith, time and eternity.'[1] It is impossible, therefore, to practise casework without being involved in relationship, since this is the means by which the goal is achieved.

The use of relationship implies a belief in personality and an assumption that the real need of human beings is only met in personal encounter. Science and technology can confer many benefits on mankind, but fundamentally human need can only be met by another person. When, for instance, disaster hit the Welsh mining village of Aberfan and one hundred and eleven of its children were killed by the landslide of a tip, no one knew at first what to do to help in such a situation. When an appeal was made to the world for money, this was no desire to exploit tragedy, but merely the usual reaction to the kind of disaster mining communities are used to in which the breadwinner is killed. Grief cannot be healed by money, but at least money can help to allay some of the other anxieties and uncertainties that come with the loss of the breadwinner. In the case of Aberfan, however, very few men were killed. The victims were mainly the A and B stream of the Junior School, boys and girls of nine and ten years old. To offer money in exchange for a child is pathetically inadequate. One man saw what was needed. A doctor who had specialized in studying the problems of grief went to Aberfan and succeeded in persuading the authorities that the only answer to bereavement is a person. A social worker was appointed and understood her role so well that although she started activities like play groups for the children in bereaved families, she concentrated mainly on becoming involved with the people of Aberfan. Nothing could bring the children back but the wounds could be helped to heal by the understanding concern and support of another person. Social workers are not often called in to dramatic situations like this but it only highlights what every social worker sees as his job: to establish a relationship with the person and from that standpoint try to set in motion the processes which will solve his problem or alleviate his need.

Relationship is so important to casework that it is necessary to investigate its nature more carefully. To some people it is a relatively simple matter. It is thought to be enough that another human being is physically present, and no special skill or technique is required. For this school of thought it is immaterial what is said or done so long as another person is present in the situation. On the other hand, there is a school of thought in casework that is based on Freudian psychology and so is strongly analytically orientated. For this school the relationship can only be explained in terms of transference. Freudian psychology is primarily concerned with the first five years of life and the emotional experiences of the child during that time. These experiences lay down the pattern that will determine the child's reaction to all other subsequent situations in later life. The caseworker, according to this view, plays the role of father or mother with the client behaving more or less as he behaved in childhood. The relationship therefore is determined not so much by the present situation as by the childhood experiences of the client, and the help of the caseworker consists in giving insight into the meaning of these transferences, so that the client has more understanding of himself in his situation of need. This interpretation is in fact the prerogative of the analytical psychologist, and there has from the beginning been controversy about the way in which a caseworker uses relationship. Psychiatric social workers tend to accept more of the analytical basis and to talk more readily of transference, while other caseworkers may insist emphatically that they are not in any way involved in analytical work.

Paul Halmos, in *The Faith of the Counsellors* [2] has presented a very strong argument against the idea that analytical work is done by counsellors. He maintains that in essence the relationship of anyone in a helping situation is based on concern. The vital ingredient that helps the person in need is love, and Paul Halmos believes that however much it is dressed up in psychological or scientific jargon, and whatever technique is employed, the fact remains that all anyone can offer and all anyone can receive is love.

The difficulty of such a definition is that the word love has so many different meanings. To some it implies only the human relationship between the sexes, to others it is primarily an emotion, a pleasant warm feeling of general goodwill, and to yet others love is a heavenly gift not to be confused with any human feeling but significant only in a religious context. This latter has something of the element of the general goodwill in it, but it is spiritualized and looked upon as a singular state of mind, achieved only by the very religious, unknown and unrecognizable to the uninitiated. It is interesting that while St Paul thought it necessary to define love, Jesus did not, and in the gospels he neither proves the existence of God nor explains the meaning of love. Apparently the only debatable point was not how to love, but whom to love; once the question of the neighbour had been settled it was assumed one knew what to do.

It is with this question, 'Who is my neighbour?', that casework is concerned. The answer to the question as it is framed by casework, 'What is relationship?', is most dramatically and inescapably answered by the Rumanian writer Petru Dumitriu in his novel *Incognito*.[3] In this book the author describes the terrible pilgrimage of a boy who runs away from his comfortable well-to-do middle-class home in Rumania, in order to be a hero. He fights first against the Russians and then with them as a communist, but all the time the suffering which men inflict on one another makes him question why men should behave like this. He decides that it is only possible when one can say 'you are not my brother'. This is how we persecute the Jews, people of a different colour from ourselves, men of other creeds or from other social classes; we deny that there is anything between us. The hero comes to see that the great fallacy is that we are innocent and the other, the enemy, is guilty. We tell ourselves that those who are weak or conquered or just different have nothing in common with us and are not our brothers. Sebastian, the hero, ends his pilgrimage when he learns that though a man may not be good or honest or brave, he is none the less a human being, a neighbour and a brother. In the most humiliating and agonizing circumstances of imprisonment and torture he learns the secret of love which is not a feeling nor, at heart, even a deed; it is before all else an attitude. It is the attitude that, when a man lies injured in the road between Jerusalem and Jericho, accepts the victim as a brother without noticing whether he is black or white, Jew or Gentile, a drug addict or a millionaire. It is so simple that few people have the patience to listen to it, but want to go on to something more complicated and obscure.

Yet the Rumanian writer was right; it is an attitude that is not obtained easily or naturally, but evolves only from our encounter at the depths with the reality of life, a wrestling with oneself and with God, out of which one cannot come unscathed. Sebastian's pilgrimage involved the horrors of war and revolution, which opened his eyes to what men do to one another. Somehow we all have to discover for ourselves that we are not innocent and that therefore all men are our brothers. The temptation to believe in our own innocence explains the cruelties of religious wars and persecutions. When Christianity is mistakenly believed to be about self-righteousness and not about love then it is possible for the 'saved' to say of almost everyone else, 'this is not my brother'. The result is the terrible travesty of Christianity that can fight wars, torture, exclude, condemn and live in a self-congratulating ghetto. The church has only itself to blame when it is unwanted and disregarded; it has said for so long 'these are not my brothers', that the world thankfully believes the church and has thrown off an elder brother who is interested only in his own possessions and concerns. If we lost the Bible and kept only the parables of the Good Samaritan and the Prodigal Son, we would still have the essential heart of what Jesus was and said and did. To the world it must seem as if the church has jealously guarded the literal meaning of every word in the Bible except those two parables.

Casework does not express its theory of relationship in theological terms, but this is the basis of it. It is a confrontation with another person who may be congenial and pleasant or hostile, ugly and repulsive, who may be familiar and receptive or a foreigner whose very ways of thought and behaviour, as well as his words, are incomprehensible. This confrontation is not merely a facing of the other person from a safe distance but in some way a meeting that involves contact. Sometimes this meeting can best be achieved by touching, as St Francis kissed the lepers to establish a meeting point with them. The lonely, the frightened, the confused, who cannot be reached by words, may sometimes understand a hand holding theirs, as once in childhood their hands were held to prevent them from falling. This is not the only way, nor does this in itself necessarily imply contact, but whether words, touch or an emotional response is used, the relationship is established when the other person knows that he exists, and exists not as the stranger but as a brother. One may help people from a distance, over the barrier of a wall, but one cannot establish a relationship through the Berlin Wall of non-acceptance. I may sort out people's housing problems, adjust their pensions, arrange home help, write their letters and earn their gratitude for these services, but I am not a caseworker unless I do more than this. These services are the means by which I say, 'You are my brother.' This is the dual nature of casework and its affinity to the gospel ministry. It cannot say in words alone, you are my brother, and pass by on the other side. On the other hand good works which may be done in patronage or even contempt of the recipient are not enough either. The service is both the expression of the brotherhood and the means by which the essential relationship is established.

In every sphere the caseworker is dealing with people who in one respect are different from him; he is well and the other is sick; he is sane and the other is mad; he is law-abiding and the other is a criminal; he is solvent and the other is in debt; he can mange to live in today's society, the other cannot. Relationship is not established by ignoring this difference or pretending it does not exist. Nor can the caseworker become sick or mad, inadequate or a felon in order to be like the other. Some way has to be found that forges a bond between them without it being necessary for them to be alike. Brothers are not usually identical twins, which are comparatively rare. Simone Weil made contact by discovering within herself the germ of all possible crimes. She considered this her vocation to remain, as she called it, anonymous and indistinguishable from the masses of the people. This in itself is not enough to establish a relationship, however. In *Gravity and Grace*[4] Simone Weil puts it more clearly and insists that she, in common with everyone else, is not what she imagines herself to be, and suggests that this knowledge is forgiveness. Sebastian in *Incognito* finds, too, that this is what he has been looking for and that his suffering is forcing him to the point where all he can do is love and forgive. His search for meaning ended in the discovery that the world only had meaning when he bestowed meaning on it through love and forgiveness.

The word forgiveness is unacceptable today to many people, for if it is defined in orthodox theological terms, it either has no relevant meaning or is distasteful. It is not just that many people do not feel forgiven, but that they do not accept the validity of a credit and debit view of God and fail to see what this sort of forgiveness has to do with the hard facts of the business of living. To many people Paul Tillich's[5] definition of forgiveness as acceptance strikes a chord and answers a need where the traditional definition of forgiveness has ceased to do so. It would seem artificial if relationship were explained in terms of forgiveness, each person forgiving the other for what he is, the one forgiving the other his health and prosperity, sanity and good conduct, and the other forgiving him his sickness, his madness, his poverty or his crime. Yet substitute the word acceptance and this is what happens. It is an acceptance on both sides, and fundamentally, casework training is an attempt to help the worker to achieve this acceptance. Knowledge in the purely intellectual sense cannot bring this about, but without knowledge it can rarely be accomplished. This is the great illusion of the church today, that if men are trained in theology and philosophy they are then equipped to communicate these ideas to other people and minister to them. In order to relate to other people one needs basically to know not ideas but people. This entails not merely a study of human nature but also knowledge of the society which has moulded men, and in the process both studies must be translated into self-knowledge. One does not automatically acquire forgiveness, acceptance and relationship because one has studied psychology, sociology or anthropology, but if one is intent on learning, then this knowledge may prepare the way and make it possible for one to begin to learn casework.

The learning is not finished with the end of training. The caseworker goes on learning relationship as long as he is practising casework. Every individual has something to teach, since in so far as he is different, he requires to be met in a different way. One generalizes and classifies for convenience but is brought back to individuality by the person who says, 'But I am not other people who have this experience. I am myself and no one else has been "me" before, even in this situation.' One learns by success in difficult situations, the unrewarding, unapproachable and hopeless who are met and helped; and above all one learns through failure, the missed opportunities seen too late, the people to whom no word was spoken, who were never met or known, the rejection too easily accepted, the appeal that was misunderstood, ignored or forgotten. Through all these one comes to see oneself more clearly and so learns more about the need for forgiveness, and the possibility of giving and receiving acceptance.

This definition of casework as a relationship has been criticized notably by Barbara Woolton in her book *Social Science and Social Pathology*. She finds the description of the relationship quite incredible. 'It might well be thought that the social worker's best, indeed perhaps her only, chance of achieving aims at once so intimate and so ambitious would be to marry her client.'[6] She not only finds the language of social casework incredible but frankly unacceptable. 'It can be presumed that the lamentable arrogance of the language in which contemporary social workers describe their activities is not generally matched by the work they do: otherwise it is hardly credible that they would not constantly get their faces slapped.'[7] She maintains that the social worker is essentially a provider of practical help, doing for the poor what the secretary or paid assistant does for the well-to-do, and the chief requirements are 'good manners, ability and willingness to listen, and efficient methods of record keeping'.[8]

It is easy to caricature the caseworker who offers insight when the crying need is for money to pay the rent. The fact is that the caseworker is a hybrid creature. He is not a public assistance officer under the old Poor Law, whose sole function was to assess need and provide financial assistance where necessary. This dual nature is illustrated by the results of the 1963 Children's Act, which allowed children's departments to take preventive action by giving financial aid to families in need. In some cases the department has become associated with the payment of rent arrears and electricity bills and it is even said that the social security refuse to give aid until families have first applied to the children's department. It was not the intention of the Act that the functions of social security should be taken over but that the giving of aid quickly should be done to prevent, for instance, the break-up of a family through eviction for non-payment of rent. The two functions of a social worker, the practical and the personal, are so closely related that his role becomes distorted if either is omitted or emphasized to the exclusion of the other, and he becomes either a civil servant or a psychotherapist.

NOTES

1. F. P. Biestek, *The Casework Relationship*, Allen & Unwin, new ed. 1967, foreword.

2. Paul Halmos, *The Faith of the Counsellors*, Constable 1965.

3. Petru Dumitriu, *Incognito*, Collins 1964.

4. Simone Weil, *Gravity and Grace*, Routledge & Kegan Paul 1953.

5. Paul Tillich, *The Shaking of the Foundations*, SCM Press 1949 and Penguin Books 1962.

6. Barbara Woolton, *Social Science and Social Pathology*, Allen & Unwin 1959, p. 273.

7. *Ibid.*, p.279.

8. *Ibid.*, p.291.

3 The Theory of Casework: (i) Understanding Man

Casework theory begins with an attempt to answer the psalmist's question: 'What is man?' Dietrich Bonhoeffer wrestled with the same problem in prison when he wrote his poem 'Who am I?' It is when one asks this question as he did in genuine bewilderment and in desperate need to know the answer, that one is ready for the search for knowledge that may lead to that self-awareness which underlies all deep understanding of others.

There are many points from which one may start but in this space age it may be argued with Teilhard de Chardin that 'the truth of man is the truth of the universe for man'.[1] Neil Armstrong's 'one short step' has altered the perspective for mankind beyond any going back. For the non-scientist it has hitherto been possible to have little sense of the reality of the stars and to view them as not much more than a picturesque backcloth for man's activities. Our very vocabulary reveals our true belief about the universe when we use phrases like, 'It's all moonshine.' Now moon dust is laboratory material and space travel no longer a flight of fancy. It would seem logical, therefore, that today some knowledge of the tremendous world in which we live should precede an attempt to understand what is man.

In another book, *Le Milieu Divin*, Teilhard de Chardin poses the question, 'Where are the roots of our being?' He answers the question by saying: 'In the first place they plunge back and down into the unfathomable past. How great is the mystery of the first cells which were one day animated by the breath of our souls.'[2] It may seem to some people irrelevant to start a study of mankind with an examination of cell structure, but it is debatable whether our explorations into space will in the end have as far-reaching results as the experiments that have been carried out into the nature of the cell. It may well be that the future of mankind is after all not in the hands of the space scientists but with the geneticists. One of the facts that the study of genetics has revealed is the uniqueness of the individual. The genetic code of every person is different in some degree so that everyone is uniquely himself. This gives a basis in scientific fact to the belief of the caseworker in the value of the individual. Some knowledge, therefore, of the genetic code and some understanding of the part this plays in determining human nature is essential if one is to begin with the very roots of man's existence.

Traditionally, casework theory of man has been concerned with 'the unfathomable past' in a rather different sense from that which interested Teilhard de Chardin; not with man's biological past but with his unconscious mind. The greatest influence on casework theory in the last forty to fifty years has been that of Freudian psychology. In fact it would be true to say that casework's answer to the psalmist's question would often be: 'Freudian man'. Freud's theory of the nature of man is based on his discovery of the unconscious mind.[3] Before Freud it was assumed that to talk of mental activity as unconscious was a contradiction in terms and his scientific opponents today would call it not so much a discovery as an invention. Freud's experience with neurotic patients convinced him that consciousness is only one aspect of our mental processes. He believed that his neurotic patients were suffering from memories of traumatic events which had been pushed out of immediate memory, but were still causing fear and anxiety. At first Freud used hypnosis to recall these forgotten experiences, but not everyone can be hypnotized, so he developed his method of free association. He believed that the memories were repressed and held down in the unconscious, and he claimed to release them by making the patient relax, and instructing him to rid his mind of all criticisms and allow ideas to come freely. In this way the patient revealed his hidden fears and anxieties. Psycho-analysis is used to describe various forms of treatment, but in fact, it is only correctly used to describe the technique of free association. Freud also used his patient's dreams as a means of understanding the unconscious. Indeed he called dreams 'the royal road' to the unconscious and when asked how one could become a psycho-analyst he would reply, 'By studying one's own dreams'. In fact nothing was too trivial for Freud to use in his interpretation of the unconscious. In his book *The Psychopathology of Everyday Life* he declared that there are no accidents as we generally understand the word, but that all small faulty actions, stumbling, slips of the tongue and pen, are acts revealing the thoughts and wishes in the unconscious. For anyone who understands them these slips are not trivial but revealing.

The mind of Freudian man consists of the Id, the Ego and the Super Ego. The Id is everything that is present in the mind at birth and that is inherited. It is the core of man's being and the home of the instincts. Freud thought there were two instincts, Eros and Thanatos, life and death. His Thanatos is often misquoted as a death-wish. Thanatos for Freud was the desire to return to a former state, which he interpreted as a desire to return to inorganic matter. Atomic theory makes nonsense of this today, for we can no longer think of matter as dead. The Id has no direct contact with the outer world but is only accessible through the medium of another part of the mind. It is ruled by the pleasure principle. By pleasure Freud meant the absence of pain or dissatisfaction, and the aim of the Id is to get rid of unpleasure by having its wants satisfied. The Id knows no other rule than the obtaining of this state of pleasure as quickly as possible.

Yet needs can only be satisfied by contact with the outside world, so that the Id needs the help of that part of the mind Freud called the Ego. He thought of the Ego as a cortical layer, capable of receiving stimulation from the outer world. The Ego is dominated by the reality principle and its task is self-preservation. If the Id had its way destruction would be the result. The Ego balances the claims of the outside world with those of the Id within and has to induce the Id to postpone its claims, modify its aims or even, in return for compensation, give them up altogether. If the Id is the driving force of the vehicle, then the Ego is the steering. It has the difficult role of appeaser of both the world and the Id and may break down under the strain.

The Super Ego is very like what theology calls the conscience. It is an internalized set of rules and standard of conduct. It can appear to the Ego as a strict punishing father, and neurotic illnesses may be the result of an overwhelming sense of guilt, which can only be satisfied if punished by illness. The Super Ego was thought by Freud to be the end product of the first five years of development. Freud thought that man was originally an animal that came to sexual maturity in five years. In the development of evolution this process went into cold storage and only came into full maturity after a latency period. He believed that all essential development still takes part in the first five years of life, and this determines our responses to all situations in later life. According to Freud our sexual development starts at birth and he labels the stages from the areas of the body from which pleasure is derived. Thus the first year of life is the oral stage, in which all satisfaction is through the mouth. The next stage is the anal stage during which toilet training takes place, and when pleasure is transferred to the anal area. The third stage, roughly between three and five years, is the genital stage. It is during this period that Freud thought the Oedipus complex was resolved. Freud knew only the patriarchal society in which he lived and was ignorant of other cultures, so that he mistook a local phenomenon for a universal feature of human nature. He thought that all boys at this stage are sexually attracted to their mothers and hate their fathers as rivals. This situation is made more threatening by a fear of castration and cannot be endured, so the boy relinquishes the mother as a love object and accepts the father as a model for future manhood. The Super Ego, Freud thought, developed out of this conflict, as a standard and an ideal, and the fiercer the conflict the harsher the Super Ego. Freud did not understand women, and admitted as much, but thought that a similar process must take place in women. As with boys, the driving force to compel them to relinquish the love object is partly fear and partly a desire to please. Once the Oedipus complex has been resolved our essential development is complete, and all subsequent development is determined by the way we dealt with this experience.

Casework theory has been heavily dependent on Freud's view of man, and it underlies a good deal of current practice. Some textbooks seem to assume that this is man and that complete understanding of the mystery of mankind can be achieved by close attention to the first five years as analysed by Freud. Freud, however, was limited both by his own social environment of a patriarchial society with rigid social standards, and by the knowledge available at that time, especially in the field of anthropology. A study of other cultures than those of Western Europe makes it plain, for instance, that the Oedipus complex, which Freud taught was a universal factor in human development, does not exist in those people who grow up in a culture with a different family pattern. It has also been disputed that all human development is determined by the experiences of the first five years, and Freud's insistence that the core of our being is sexual was contested by his most gifted disciple, Carl Gustav Jung.[4]

Jung could not accept this answer to the question, 'What is man?', so he left Freud in order to find his own answer. Jung was more interested in the inside of experiences than the outside, and after his break with Freud he pursued his own interest in the images that lie behind our emotions. By exploring his own dreams and fantasies he came to the conclusion that as well as a personal unconscious there is a racial unconscious, in which are stored the archetypal images that are common to man. Jung was very interested in myth and legend, and thought that the common features that appear in myths and folklore from widely separated places could be explained by his theory of archetypes. In the personal unconscious he suggested that everyone has a 'persona', a mask that is the role we play, because society expects it, but that is not really an individual. He also suggested that we each have a 'shadow', a lower self that is the primitive uncontrolled part of us. He pointed out that we all postulate the existence of the shadow when we say, 'I don't know what came over me,' or 'I wasn't myself when I did it.' He also suggested that our unreasonable dislikes of other people may really be a dislike of our own shadow seen in another person. He thought that this was shown in a collective sense in a witch hunt when the victim was a substitute for the pursuers' darker selves. Jung believed that mental health depends on the acceptance of our shadow, and that unexpected outbreaks, especially of sexual misdemeanours, in hitherto respectable people, are the result of refusal to face the shadow and rejection of it. He believed that the unconscious shadow could become conscious in dreams. He realized that it needs moral courage to face oneself but once accomplished, this makes it possible for change to occur, whereas if it is ignored the shadow may completely overwhelm the personality. Mob riots are the work of the shadow, and the only cure is acceptance of ourselves as we are. Laurens van der Post in *Venture into the Interior*[5] suggests that the whole colour question and our attitude to it comes from the existence of this dark self and our ambivalance towards it, so that we reject it and yet pursue it, as we reject the black man and yet are fascinated by Africa, the 'dark continent'.

In the collective unconscious Jung thought that there existed the elements of both sexes. Psychologically he thought that we all have both sexes, that is, a man has a female unconscious and a woman a male. He called the female archetype the anima, which is built up of the age-old experience of man and woman and does not represent the character of an individual woman. Through contacts with actual people this image becomes conscious and may be projected first on a man's mother and then on women who attract him. This is the reason for inexplicable love affairs and some disastrous marriages. The anima may be of great value to a man, as for instance in the cult of the Virgin, or Dante's 'Beatrice', but she may also be disastrous like the Lorelei or La Belle Dame sans Merci. The woman has in her unconscious the animus which is a collective image of man. This too will influence her relationships. It is interesting to notice in literature how the animus may appear in a woman's writings, under such widely different guises as Heathcliff and Lord Peter Wimsey. Jung thought that a woman could be ruled by her animus and then would be critical, harsh and authoritative and tending to speak always about 'everybody' and 'people' as final authorities. The animus can be like an assembly of fathers or dignitaries who lay down the law. On the other hand, if a woman recognizes the animus and uses it, it may make her search for knowledge and truth and be the source of purposeful activity. Other symbols that may appear in dreams or fantasies are the Wise Old Man, and the Great Mother. It is not difficult to find examples of men who have believed themselves to be possessed of a power and indeed have made others believe in them too. Hitler is an example of this. Most people also will have met women possessed by the archetype of the Great Mother who have believed themselves to be endowed with extraordinary gifts for loving and helping other people, and can yet be most destructive, since all who come under her influence are her children and are made to remain helpless and dependent. This can be most destructive to the personality of those so subjected.

Jung thought that man could be possessed by these archetypes, and sometimes this possession would give the feeling of being a superman. This is an illusion, and disaster will inevitably follow. The only way to true humanity is through humility before the various aspects of our personality, to achieve acceptance of what we are. When we can truly see ourselves and accept what we see, then it is possible for a new centre of personality to emerge, which Jung calls the self. This is not the Ego of Freud for it includes both the conscious and the unconscious and it draws together the many discordant parts of the personality, good and bad, male and female. This self is achieved in maturity and can only be reached by a considerable struggle. It brings a feeling of oneness with life and of reconciliation with it, so that it can be accepted as it is. Jung saw the growth of the self in many of his patients. For some dreams of a child symbolized the beginning of this new experience, but most often the symbol was the pattern known as the mandala, a circle, square or the four-armed cross. This symbol is one of the oldest religious symbols and is found in many forms. Jung found it in the dreams and in the paintings of his patients. Jung himself tells of dreams he had of a square with a fountain in the centre, or an island with flowers and trees. Jung called the process of developing the self individuation, and believed that in this process the personality is liberated, healed and transformed, so that while it becomes fully individual, it is released from being merely individualistic.

Jung adds a dimension to the understanding of man that is lacking in Freud. Most especially he offers an understanding of the mature person who may not be needing psychiatric treatment but who is looking for guidance in the process of living as an adult and needs to understand his present experience. An attempt to help man, not with his unfathomable past but with his incomprehensible present, was made by Freud's other famous disciple, Alfred Adler, who also broke away and founded his own school of Individual Psychology. His book *What Life Should Mean to You* can be understood by the non-specialist and those without much knowledge of psychology can read it with profit and interest.[6]

Adler taught that all of us have a meaning in life, which is developed in the first few years, and which is revealed in all our actions. Neurotic behaviour can be described quite simply as mistaken meaning. His aim was to teach people better meanings. The true meaning of life, he taught, is to contribute to the whole. He did not believe in determinism, as Freud did, nor in the trauma of early experience. He believed that we are self-determined and make out of our experiences what we choose. He was a great believer in the training of children and thought the worst thing that could happen to a child was not for it to be neglected, but for it to be spoiled. His theory of mistaken meanings is bound up with his theory of inferiority. He thought that children with imperfect organs, diseases or infirmities were, unless correctly trained, liable to have mistaken ideas of the meaning of life. The feeling of inferiority is in everyone; we only differ in how we deal with it. It can be a challenge and it is the cause of all improvements in life, since there is always something bigger than ourselves. The inferiority complex is not a complaint; it is our common lot and the only difference is the courage with which we seek to improve the situation, or the way we evade the issue. If we have not been taught to face life with courage we still struggle, but only to become superior, and the situation remains unaltered, and so do our feelings of inferiority. The inferiority complex, in fact, expresses our conviction that the problem cannot be solved. Adler thought that the Oedipus complex, so far from being universal as Freud believed, was only a refusal on the part of some people to meet the problem of love. Adler tried to show people that neurotic struggles were on the useless side of life and that what was needed was to transfer their efforts to the useful side. To be useful Adler thought that actions should be directed towards interest in others and to co-operation. If a man could be a good friend to all men and make his contribution by useful work and a happy marriage, Adler believed he would never feel inferior to others or defeated by them. He would feel at home in the world and equal to all his difficulties. The task of man, in Adler's view, is to take responsibility for solving the problems of work, of associations with fellow human beings and of love and marriage in a co-operative way.

Study of the many theories of the development of man only makes it clearer that there is no one direct answer to the question, 'What is man?' The understanding that is the basis for casework practice has to be gathered in many places. Freud, Jung, Adler all provide insights from a certain standpoint but much more is needed to fill out the picture of human development. One study that has played an important part in determining the way children should be treated is John Bowlby's work on maternal deprivation.[7]

His research into the long-term effects on children of the lack of a mother-figure during the early years has not merely been of interest to psychologists but has had a practical influence on the treatment of children, especially those in hospital or institutions. Bowlby's contention was that complete deprivation of a mother-figure could result in a personality defect that is usually called psychopathy.

45

The subjects he studied were shown to be incapable of forming any deep and stable relationship and were lacking in moral responsibility, so that they were often engaged in criminal activity. Bowlby called the group he studied 'the affectionless thieves'. This research has helped to outline something of the nature and cause of psychopathy. Even more, his study of babies and children in institutions has shown how these children may be backward both physically and mentally, compared with children having a normal family life. When these children were taken out of the institutions and given the loving care of a mother-substitute, they began to make progress and catch up with their contemporaries. In the first years of life all children need a mother-figure to love them and take pleasure in their progress if they are to develop normally. Some of Bowlby's findings have been disputed but he has at least done much to alter our practice of having children in hospital without permitting the mother to visit. Now free visiting is common practice, and many hospitals make provision for the mother of a small child to be admitted with him. Nurseries are run on more personal lines and more effort is made to establish a relationship with the child. Whenever possible children's departments board children out in families to avoid the institutionalization of young children. Bowlby's plea for the prevention of maternal deprivation by helping families in difficulty before they break up and the children are taken into care, is still an ideal and not yet universal practice.

One of the failings of much of casework theory is that it is centred on the first few years of life. Important as these years are there are many other experiences in human life that need to be understood if man is to be comprehended. Man develops even after adulthood is reached, and middle age as well as old age has its problems. In addition to these normal experiences some people face illness, physical or mental, and disability of various kinds. Blindness, deafness and physical handicap all have a profound influence on a person's life, whether they are congenital or acquired later through illness or accident. One of the important effects is the attitude of other people to any form of disability. This has been given careful study by Goffman in his book *Stigma*.[8] He has made it clear that a person's attitude to his disability is inevitably coloured by society's labelling of him as at best different and at worst a freak.

To understand man as fully as possible it is necessary to know something of what it means to be ill. It is not so much medical knowledge that is required as a grasp of the social aspects of illness, the current attitudes to it and the effects of certain diseases on family relationships, the work situation and social life in general. Cancer, for instance, is a word so charged with feelings of fear and dread that many doctors never use it to the patient. Relatives may have fantasies of the patient in agonies of pain and a tortuous death scene which impel them to resist any suggestion that the patient should come home from hospital. These fears often lie behind an adamant refusal to care for a case of terminal cancer. Coronary thrombosis is a social disease in that it may affect the roles of husband and wife, if one partner is suffering from it. If the husband is the victim it may mean a change of job or in some cases a reversal of roles so that the wife becomes the breadwinner. Tuberculosis is another complaint that can have far-reaching effects on the patient, quite apart fom the actual physical symptoms of the disease. The history of TB as a fatal disease can make young people terrified of it and even fatalistic as they believe they are doomed, however much reassurance is given as to the efficiency of modern treatment. The family are sure to be affected, as they will be examined as contacts. Sometimes employers panic at the news that an employee has TB, and will wonder what it will mean to the other workmen, and whether he should forbid them to visit the hospital. Some skin complaints can cause social difficulties,

47

not only of embarrassment to the sufferer but also other people may wrongly believe the complaint to be infectious and may refuse to work with him.

Better understanding of man has produced insight into the nature and treatment of mental illness. More people are now treated in hospital because symptoms are recognized and understood more readily, drugs are available and admission to hospital, since the 1959 Mental Health Act, is now as informal as admission to any other hospital. The custodial aspect has been reduced to a minimum and the preoccupation with legal provisions to safeguard the rights of those who might be wrongly committed to hospital has given way to a concern that those who could benefit from treatment should get it with the minimum of formality. There is no doubt that much of the stigma of the lunatic asylum still remains, and both in their social life and in employment former patients may find prejudice that hinders their return to normal life and work. Although many mental conditions can be greatly alleviated if not cured, problems still remain. The 1959 Act advocated community care as the ideal treatment for mental patients. This has not yet been fully explored and can only be carried out to a very limited extent. Some studies of mental illness even suggest that return to the family, so far from being the ideal treatment, means sending the patient back to the situation which caused illness. In particular R. D. Laing[9] has explored the theory that schizophrenia originates in the family patterns of behaviour, and is the patient's attempt to live in an intolerable situation. Much more study and much more education of families are needed before we can claim to have a thorough understanding of man when he is mentally sick, and can develop the idea of community care to replace hospital care.

So far man has been discussed as an individual as if he existed as an isolated unit in society. Yet his very physical nature, which imposes a long dependent childhood on him, ensures that he cannot live without others. The myth of the baby brought up by wolves or apes is not based on reality. If the baby survived physically it would not grow up into anything recognizable as a human being. The question 'What is man?' can never be completely answered by any study that sees him in isolation.

NOTES

1. Teilhard de Chardin, *Human Energy*, Collins 1969.
2. Teilhard de Chardin, *Le Milieu Divin*, Collins 1960, p. 30.
3. Sigmund Freud, *Beyond the Pleasure Principle. The Ego and the Id*, Hogarth Press 1950.
Two Short Accounts of Psycho-Analysis, Penguin Books 1962.
4. Carl Gustav Jung, *Memories, Dreams and Reflections*, Collins 1963.
5. Laurens van der Post, *Venture into the Interior*, Hogarth Press 1952.
6. Alfred Adler, *What Life Should Mean to You*, Allen & Unwin 1962.
7. John Bowlby, *Child Care and the Growth of Love*, Penguin Books 1953.
8. E. Goffman, *Stigma*, Penguin Books 1968.
9. R. D. Laing and A. Esterson, *Sanity, Madness and Family*, Tavistock Publications 1964.

4   The Theory of Casework: (ii) Understanding Society

It is no longer possible to hold to the romantic idea that man had only to be abandoned on a desert island as an infant to grow up noble and pure, intelligent and honest, because he is uncorrupted by society. In fact it now seems fairly certain that a baby only becomes a person in contact with other people. For many years man has been thought of as an individual, who reluctantly became a social creature in order to survive. Rousseau's *Social Contract* may be criticized philosophically, but the underlying assumption that man is alien to society has been taken for granted. The individualist view of nature, 'red in tooth and claw', has not been seriously questioned, and it has been accepted that society is a necessary evil imposed on individualist man.

Recently theories have changed, Nature is viewed completely differently and is now seen as one vast society. From the very simplest forms of life to the highest there is society, which is more than just our environment, but our very nature. Society is not only imposed on us from without but exists within us. The balance of nature is a phrase that is only just beginning to have meaning for us, when its sinister implications are becoming obvious. As scientific techniques change vegetation and population of insects, birds and animals, we are realizing how much of nature is an interdependent society, in which one need only remove one element to upset the whole balance of half a dozen other elements in an endless chain reaction of consequences.

Society therefore is something that belongs to man's inherent nature and one does not need to question further why it has developed.

One may, however, wonder why man has elaborated the structure of society and why he has developed such complex civilizations. Even the most primitive society known to us is very different from the simple social life of apes, and one needs to ask why man should have developed society in this way. Freud believed that it was due to the 'incest barrier', that is, that man had to form groups within which it was possible to marry. This begs the question as it offers no explanation of the incest barrier, which has no biological significance. Another suggestion is that basically society depends on economic advantage, that is, a division of labour, so that at its simplest one need not be so alert or have sole care of offspring. Another theory is that man's prime need is for company. Man is not gregarious in that he needs company for its own sake, but he needs other people to satisfy his deep needs of being liked, loved and admired. Man has a dual need of having preferences for other people and of being preferred by others. He needs love, not only throughout his long childhood but also during his whole life. His need for admiration is thought by some to be the real basis for society: man's attention to what other people think.

Robert Ardrey in *African Genesis*[1] has produced the theory that man enters society in order to defend a territory. He maintains that the historical evidence of our remote ancestors points to the fact that man is basically a territorial animal, and that it is his nature to defend a territory by aggression. In this theory society is the means of survival for a creature who is always physically vulnerable. The instinct to own a territory and defend it is deeper than the sex instinct, according to Ardrey, and all civilization is really about man's constant preoccupation with the development of the weapon. His constant dream is of the superior weapon and nothing

51

ever really diverts him from this purpose. Ardrey also considers man to be a bad-weather animal, who achieves his development in conditions of stress. Man becomes himself under the challenge of changing conditions, and the society he builds is his response to the challenge. Ardrey suggests that the theme of *West Side Story* is not one of juvenile delinquency but of our natural human instincts: territory, the gang, loyalty to one's own social group and fierce antagonism to the territorial neighbours.

However society came into being and whatever its source, the fact remains that it is the environment of every human being and man cannot be understood without some understanding of society also. Every society differs, and has its standards or norms. The word 'normal' has rather diverse meanings. On the one hand it is often used as if the ideal is the norm, and the more one approaches the ideal the more normal one is. In this sense it is sometimes claimed that no one is normal. On the other hand the norm is often used for the average, so that the normal is that which is not outstanding in any way, not too intelligent or beautiful or healthy. Normal is also used to mean natural, in the sense of that which is biologically determined. Something of all these meanings is included in a social norm. All societies tend to think that their standards are natural, inevitable and the very best. A study of anthropology soon reveals how comparative most norms are, and that normality to a large extent depends on culture.

One of the most revealing studies was that done by Margaret Mead on adolescence in Samoa. [2] The starting point for this study was the assumption that adolescence is normally a time of stress and rebellion, of emotional upheaval and strain. Margaret Mead studied a group of adolescents in Samoa and found that they exhibited none of the turbulent characteristics that we take for granted. She therefore concluded that, so far from being a biological feature of adolescence, the stress that we associate with it is the result of our culture. A 'normal' adolescent, therefore, is one who behaves as his society expects him to behave, and that behaviour may vary tremendously from culture to culture. Margaret Mead has also shown by her studies of different peoples that our norms of male and female are culturally imposed. The so-called dominance of the male and submissiveness of the female is reversed in some societies, and it is the men who sit at home, gossip, have the vapours, burst into tears and are petty, jealous and emotional, while the women go out to work, are good at business, are logical, hard and unemotional, stable and industrious. The female of our society is not so much a biological specimen, as the product of years of conditioning by western culture, as Simone de Beauvoir pointed out in her book *The Second Sex*.[3]

Ruth Benedict in *Patterns of Culture*[4] describes three tribes with very different norms: the Zuni, Dobu and Kwakiutl tribes. The Zuni tribe are a ceremonious people, valuing sobriety above all other virtues. Their whole life is centred in their religion and its rich and complex ceremonial. Their ideal is the 'middle-of-the-road' man and their dislike is for any sort of excess. A normal man is quiet, pleasing, generous and very punctilious in observing the religious rites. Any man seeking leadership is liable to be condemned as a sorceror. To be normal among the Zuni is to be average and have a horror of being anything else.

The Dobu tribe, on the other hand, are very poor and their existence is so precarious that it can only be maintained by cut-throat competition. They are characterized by jealousy and suspicion, fierce ownership and treachery. The ideal man is the one who has succeeded by cheating another of his place. Their culture provides elaborate techniques and opportunities for this behaviour. Their institutions exact animosity and maliciousness, and their form of thanks on receiving a gift is, 'If you now poison me, how should I repay you?' The normal man in this society is one who, in another

53

culture, would be regarded as a criminal in outlook if not in actual deeds.

The third tribe, the Kwakiutl, would in our society be regarded as mad. Their norm is unabashed megalomania. The ideal man is the one who can boast of his own possessions and his power to destroy his rivals. Property is all important to this tribe. Suicide is common, whenever anyone is shamed, and sulking is part of normal behaviour. A normal man from our society would be judged mad by the Kwakiutl, just as their ideal man would be treated for mental illness in our culture. Few people among the Kwakiutl question the norms and naturally most people believe that everyone lives in this way. All societies live by this unquestioning acceptance of their standards, and the only way that society can be understood is to look at the norms of our own and other societies and see that they are relative.

If social norms are the standards which exist in every society, then our response to the expectations which these arouse is role playing. Roles are essential in society because they tell an individual what he may do himself and what he may expect of other people. It has been suggested that one reason for the prevalence of delinquency and neurosis in our society is that, in a world of rapid social change, we do not know what roles to play or how to play them.

A role is a pattern for any particular situation and it is recognized both by the person who plays the role and by those who expect it. The medical student, for instance, has to acquire not only a vast amount of medical knowledge but also has to learn to behave like a doctor; that is, to be recognizable as a doctor. He may joke about the bedside manner, but sooner or later he will, in the words of the Sydney Carter song, 'wear the mask' of a doctor. A young officer in the army will soon begin to behave in the correct military manner and the theological student will, with his theology, acquire a dog collar and a clergyman's voice. Every child learns early to play a role. He is told that little boys do not play with dolls, and the girl is told that her role does not include football and other masculine pastimes. This role playing not only expresses the feelings and attitudes of a situation but manufactures them as well. The medical student, by acting like a doctor, comes more and more to feel like one, and children find their sexual identity by playing the male and female role. Elizabeth Barrett is an interesting example of the importance of role playing. She was brought up with her brothers and really believed she could play the same role until the time came for them to go to public school, when she found that she could not go too. She had no experience in a feminine role so she took to her bed and became an interesting invalid until Robert Browning encouraged her to try the feminine role, whereupon she was able to get up and walk, get married and travel to Italy. The tragic sequence was that she reversed the process with her son, whom she dressed as a girl, and thoroughly spoiled so that he never learned to play his masculine role in life and became a hopeless failure in society.

Usually children learn their role as easily and naturally as they learn now to address a letter. A small girl may think it is as normal to address a letter to Granny-by-the-sea, and expect everyone to know where it is, as to say, 'I'm going to be a daddy when I grow up,' or 'I shall be a fireman like John.' Very soon, however, she is proudly printing an envelope to Granny with street, town and county all correct and saying loftily to her current boy playmate, 'I shall marry you when I grow up.' She hardly realizes how she has learnt to play her role but she is already finding her place in society. It has been said that we become that as which we are address-ed, so that we acquire our identity as other people recognize it in us. This recognition is vital, if we are to maintain our role. We first learn by playing. A child plays at many roles, as he tries to discover his place in society. His own role depends very much on his acceptance by the family group, or those who are significant for him. If he is accepted here and learns his role, he can then play it confidently in the larger world.

One does not perhaps realize how essential a part of life role playing is, unless for some reason one's role is drastically altered. This is clearly described in the book *Black Like Me*,[5] in which the author tells how by drugs he temporarily changed the pigmentation of his skin and became black. He travelled the southern states of America and was appalled to discover how hard he found it to remember that society expected him to play a very different role from his habitual one. It was not so much that he had to act a part as that a script was forced upon him and he had no choice but to read it. This book makes clear how much we take our own and other peoples' roles for granted and how little of what we think of as typical and characteristic is in fact natural, but is imposed by the expectations of society. Black men are inferior because they have been given an inferior place in American society, and from birth they are taught to play this role, by black and white alike.

One may ask why, then, do people play roles? Although it may not be immediately obvious every society has its own controls which ensures that roles are maintained. There is always economic pressure to be reckoned with. Every job has its code of conduct and a role that must be played: failure to do so may result in the loss of the job. Most professions have very subtle ways of imposing the role, favoured by the prevailing fashion. D. H. Lawrence in *The Rainbow*[6] has a realistic account of the struggles of a young teacher to preserve her ideals and standards as a teacher, under the pressure of her colleagues to make her play the role according to accepted tradition. A nurse finds it hard to defy the standards of the hospital which decrees that she should behave in a traditional way before patients, senior staff and consultants. The working-class child going to the grammar school finds it very hard not to conform to middle-class norms, and some are forced to play two roles, one at home and one at school. We have a psychological need to be accepted by the group in which we find ourselves, so this puts pressure on us often without our being aware of the fact. Most groups use the weapons of persuasion, ridicule or disapproval to make others conform and few people can withstand this pressure. In extreme cases ostracism may be used, and to be sent to Coventry may be the cruellest punishment a group can impose. Some societies train their children by ridicule, laughing at them instead of punishing them. By one means or another everyone is induced to conform to some extent and to play a role that society can recognize.

Another way in which one may stand aside and observe society is by considering the social structures. In our particular society one may study the institution of the family, the neighbourhood or community and social class. There are a number of studies which give insight into these structures. The classic study of Bethnal Green, *Family and Kinship in East London*,[7] is a good illustration. It makes apparent the family patterns that exist in this community. The chief characteristic is the strong link that exists between the mother and daughter and that lasts as long as the mother is alive, not being weakened at all by marriage. On the contrary, the daughter's husband is expected to become part of his wife's family. It is taken for granted that he, too, will spend a great deal of time with Mum and that on all festive occasions he will be found with his wife's family and not with his own parents. Mum becomes an institution in herself, and her daughter would not dream of accepting the health visitor's or even the doctor's advice, if it contradicted Mum's store of traditional knowledge. This special pattern of the family depends on the environment and its history. Bethnal Green is a district and community with a tradition of long residence and a history of Huguenot settlements, of which the inhabitants are very proud. In this setting the family is the bridge between the individual and the community. Landlords are accustomed to Mum asking for the tenancy of a vacant house to be given to a daughter about to get married, and no one thinks of this as jumping the housing queue. That this is a purely local situation was proved when families were rehoused on a new estate in Essex. The family pattern did not, on the whole, survive the move. The young couples who settled in Essex built up a different tradition. When the first estates and new towns were built little attention was paid to the existence of family patterns and there was a tendency to found communities consisting almost entirely of young couples with children. Later, as it became clear that this is an artificial pattern, some new towns began to offer housing on the basis of relationship: parents, uncles and aunts, even grandparents of existing inhabitants were given priority in housing, in order to create a more congenial family pattern.

It is sometimes asserted today that class structures no longer exist in this country. This is obviously untrue: the structures have changed very much in this century but they have not disappeared. Any real understanding of society must take class into account. One of the difficulties of this study is that each class has its stereotyped picture of the others. Many middle-class people really believe that all the working class rehoused in new areas keep the coal in the bath. The distinction today is not really in possessions, as the working class may often own more of the symbols of affluence, but there is a great difference in attitudes.

One of the interesting studies in class is that of John and Elizabeth Newsome, *Infant Care and Urban Community*. [8] This study shows how even in the first few months of a baby's life he is subjected to influences that will form his outlook and place him in the class of his parents. The authors show how different are the principles and practice of working- and middle-class mothers in bringing up their children. Middle-class mothers tend to think of breast-feeding as a duty that must be performed, while the working-class mothers will do what is most convenient. Middle-class mothers are ashamed of the 'dummy' and will rarely admit to using it, but in the working class it is taken for granted as part of a baby's equipment. In middle-class homes mothers are ashamed if a child is not weaned by twelve months but a working-class child may have a bottle at bedtime at two or even three years old.

Another interesting study is *Education and the Working Class*,[9] by Brian Jackson and Dennis Marsden. This is a study of eighty-eight working-class children who have attended the grammar schools in Huddersfield since the Education Act of 1944, when education became free. The authors have tried to find out what happened to these pupils during their schooling. The grammar schools have a middle-class outlook and obviously the attitude of working-class children would be affected. Some pupils remembered that explicit efforts were made to wean them from their working-class backgrounds, by insisting that they dropped their former friends and discarded local activities for those at school. Some were only too happy to conform and became, as it were, militants of the middle-class way of life. Others lived a dual existence, speaking dialect at home but BBC English at school, and these emerged uneasy and unsure where they belonged. Some rebelled from the start and resisted all efforts to change them. For some, grammar school seemed to have been a disastrous failure and they had reverted to a working-class job, though even here they seemed to be a misfit. One of the most interesting questions the authors put to former grammar school pupils was, which social class they belonged to. Some forty-five of them considered they were middle class, but thirty, in spite of income and profession, insisted that they were working class. Some gave as their reason the fact that their parents were working class and it is impossible to change class. Some of those who called themselves middle class also said their parents were, too, although according to the evidence all the children came from working-class homes. A small group said that they were classless, including one, a minister, who said he was not allowed to be in any class in his profession! Most of his parishioners would certainly put him in the middle class. The authors began the book to try and find out why there is such a wastage of working-class ability, as so many children leave grammar school before the sixth form. It has, however, developed into a fascinating study of the way in which social class influences life today.

The concept of community has come to the fore in the post-war period with the extensive building programmes, especially in the new towns and redevelopment areas. Many studies of different communities are available to give an insight into the place that community plays in our lives. For instance, Hilda Jennings, in *Societies in the Making*,[10] describes an area in Bristol known as Barton Hill. This was a close-knit community that had known little change until it was designated a slum area. It was decided to rebuild on the same site in the hope of preserving the old community. The study shows how little of this end was achieved. In *Neighbourhood and Community*,[11] two areas are studied, one in Sheffield and one in Liverpool. In the Sheffield estate whole streets were moved together in an effort to retain the community. In *Family and Neighbourhood*,[12] J. Mogey compares an old and a new area in Oxford, and discovers that the people of the new estate have a suspicion of their surroundings which is expressed as a disapproval of those living in the other parts of the estate. The chief point to emerge from all these studies is how little we know what makes community and how difficult it is to preserve it. The family pattern in Bethnal Green, for instance, was broken on the Essex housing estate and the community seemed to lose its spirit as well. In Barton Hill the tall blocks of flats housed the same people, but they could no longer sit at their front doors and talk to passers-by, and all the little corner shops had disappeared and somehow with these the community went too. Community is obviously elusive and it may be that our ideal is based on a village society that is no longer relevant.

Man as a social being can be studied from other points of view. His attitudes, for instance, have been measured by the psychologists and research has been done into the way in which we influence each other and can be made to change our attitudes. Linked to this is the subject of mass influence, developed in *The Hidden Persuaders*,[13] a study of mass media and advertising, and also by William Sargant's *Battle for the Mind*,[14] which is concerned with brain-washing and conversion techniques. Such books indicate how much of our thinking and our behaviour is influenced by the society in which we live. The study of prejudice, that is of opinions which are largely without basis in reality, is also important for the understanding of man. How irrational prejudice can be was proved by one psychologist who gave students a list of peoples, and asked them to mark those against whom there is prejudice. He included such races as Jews, Japanese, Irish and two invented races who existed only in his own mind. He found that there is widespread prejudice against these non-existent people. Some psychologists have attempted to discover what sort of people are most prejudiced and whether certain forms of upbringing tend to produce prejudiced adults. Others have tried to find out how prejudice may be destroyed and have found that this is very difficult indeed. It has been suggested that an authoritarian type of personality, produced by a harsh punitive upbringing, is most liable to violent prejudice that is resistant to all propaganda. Close contact does not seem to reduce prejudice, as life in the Deep South of America or in South Africa seems to prove. Nor is it a case of mistaken information that can be corrected by education. Fundamentally, prejudice is a problem of human nature, of feeling insecure, so that a rejected group must be found on whom feelings of rejection can be projected. The essence of prejudice is that it is a bolster to self-esteem, and makes it unnecessary to face the problem of coming to terms with oneself. The only long-term solution to prejudice is an education which provides individuals with enough strength not to need the defence mechanism of prejudice.

The realization that man can only be considered as a member of society has caused some change of outlook among those concerned with social work. The exclusive interest in casework as the sphere for social workers, with its emphasis on the face-to-face relationship in the one person, is giving way to an interest in group work and community work. Group work may be no more than a labour-saving device making the most economical use of personnel by having one social worker to a group of juvenile delinquents, parents of disturbed children, patients in a mental hospital or inmates in a prison. At best, however, it recognizes the fact that the group itself may be a means of helping and healing. The Henderson Hospital, for instance, has used group work to develop the idea of a therapeutic community and this is described by Maxwell Jones in his book *Social Psychiatry in Practice*.[15] The dynamics of small groups have been explored from a number of different viewpoints with attention being paid to the attitudes to a leader, to the existence of a 'scapegoat' and the playing of roles in group. The basic assumptions of a group according to Bion[16] are flight and fight, dependency and pairing. Most studies of groups are to some extent indebted to the work of Bion and even if not all his interpretations of group phenomena can be accepted, evidence of his basic assumptions can be seen in many different sorts of groups.

Community development acknowledges both that man is a social animal and that many of his problems are social in origin and therefore need something more than an individual solution. Social workers are being encouraged to think in terms of working with neighbourhoods and groups of people, to help them to organize and make plans to decide what their needs are and how to meet them. One of the positive results from the disaster at Aberfan has been the achievement of two community development workers in the village, who have encouraged ideas and aspirations of the people themselves. The struggle to get the government to remove the tips before further calamities occurred produced natural leaders in the community. The planning made necessary by the large sum of money donated to the village has helped to develop initiative and skill both in identifying goals and attaining them. In new towns and new development areas it is now recognized that it is not enough for man to have a satisfying life as an individual but that he needs also a satisfactory environment in order to arrive at his fullest development. Those who plan the communities in which people live and are concerned with administration or health need to understand the relationship of man to his environment and to his fellow-men. The study group set up by the Gulbenkian Foundation recommended that all who have responsibility for communities should have some training. They also recommended full professional training for community workers, who should have skill to analyse social situations, skill in group and inter-group relations, and know how to co-operate both with voluntary and statutory services to make them aware of people's needs and to help them find acceptable ways of meeting them. [17]

Social casework as a method of helping people has in the past over-emphasized the individual aspect of man's nature. The balance is now being redressed. Casework has not been proved unnecessary, only inadequate to deal with all social need in every situation. It needs to be supplemented by the broader concepts of group and community work.

NOTES

1. Robert Ardrey, *African Genesis*, Collins Fontana Books 1967,
2. Margaret Mead, *Coming of Age in Samoa*, Penguin Books 1943.
3. Simone de Beauvoir, *The Second Sex*, Jonathan Cape 1953.

4. Ruth Benedict, *Patterns of Culture*, Routledge & Kegan Paul 1961.

5. J. H. Griffin, *Black Like Me*, Collins 1962.

6. D. H. Lawrence, *The Rainbow*, Penguin Books 1964.

7. M. Young and P. Willmott, *Family and Kinship in East London*, Penguin Books 1962.

8. J. and E. Newsome, *Infant Care and Urban Community*, Allen & Unwin 1963.

9. Brian Jackson and Dennis Marsden, *Education and the Working Class*, Penguin Books 1966.

10. Hilda Jennings, *Societies in the Making*, Routledge & Kegan Paul 1962.

11. *Neighbourhood and Community*, University Press of Liverpool 1954.

12. J. Mogey, *Family and Neighbourhood*, OUP 1960.

13. Vance Packard, *The Hidden Persuaders*, Penguin Books 1960.

14. W. Sargant, *Battle for the Mind*, Heinemann 1957.

15. Maxwell Jones, *Social Psychiatry in Practice*, Penguin Books 1968.

16. W. R. Bion, *Experiences in Groups*, Tavistock Publications 1961.

17. Gulbenkian Report: *Community Work and Social Change*, Longmans 1968.

5 The Sphere of Casework: The Crisis Situation

One way of defining casework is to say that it works in a crisis situation. Sometimes it is described as a problem-solving process, which is a less dramatic way of saying the same thing. This applies to ministry also, for it too is concerned with problem solving and serves at the point of crisis. This statement needs explaining today when Bonhoeffer has effectively demoted the 'God of the gaps' theology. This is precisely the vital distinction: theology and ministry are not the same thing. To minister in crises is not to assert that God is only present in crises. Bonhoeffer, on the other hand, was not trying to prove God's absence from the moment of crisis, only to re-establish a belief in his presence in all events and states of living. In his poetry he makes it clear that for him, as for many others, Christ is relevant because he knew true human living, which is inevitably a life of crisis.

Crisis may be defined in two ways. It is used in medicine to describe the turning point of an illness, the moment of danger or at least of suspense, in which the outcome of the illness is decided. The Greek root of the word, however, implies neither danger nor suspense, but simply decision, for it comes from the verb *krino*, to decide. All these shades of meaning are applicable to casework and to ministry also. In the gospels ministry is seen not as the answer to a hopeless situation, calling in God when all else has failed, but as the revelation of God's presence in a situation, waiting for something to be done. The crisis exists, not because God is unable or unwilling to help but because he is waiting for the human agent to be the answer to the problem. As the Old Testament prophets pointed out, it is not enough to sing hymns and express pious sentiments and leave the rest to God; God demands that his people do his work of justice and mercy, healing and reconciliation.

The supreme crises of all human life are the twin events of birth and death. The Christian ministry is traditionally concerned with death and the ceremonies connected with it. In fact, some hospital chaplains see their ministry entirely as an obligation to answer a call to visit a dying patient. Casework is not so much concerned with the literal physical fact of the death of the individual, but it has brought about a new understanding of the significance of death. It has shown death to be a part of life that occurs many times and in many forms. This is not to say that the caseworker is never to be found either preparing a person to face the fact of death or relatives to accept bereavement, for a medical social worker may often do both. The caseworker's idea of death, and especially of the grief and mourning associated with it, is widened to include many more situations than the actual death of a person. The feelings that are associated with death accompany many other events in life, and it is in this sort of situation that a caseworker has to operate.

A very simple definition of death is that it is essentially a sudden end to a way of life. This happens many times in the life of most people. This does not mean that every time a familiar way of life ends a caseworker is needed to see the person through the crisis; only that this is the point at which casework is relevant and may be required. The important fact is that this kind of crisis is not always recognized for what it is, and help is not therefore always available. It is, for instance, only just being realized that school leaving, even for those who can't wait to leave school, means a sudden break with a way of life that has been familiar for at least ten years. Difficulties at work, and at college or university, where life is still very different from life at school in spite of a similar learning situation, may lead to depression or anxiety states which may become sufficiently serious to need psychological help, or to delinquent behaviour which brings the young person into court. There will be a variety of factors causing this crisis, but one will be that, unnoticed and often with no guidance, the girl or boy has died a death in leaving school years behind, and is unable to manage the feelings which this has aroused. The setting up of Youth Guidance Councils recognizes this need of help for young people at this stage. It is not merely a question of vocational guidance and finding the right job but a need for sympathetic understanding of what it means to leave behind a familiar way of life. It is accepted that a child of five may howl and even resist when he is taken to school for the first time, for the mother too feels the pain of this situation. The closeness of the years at home is ended, and she experiences the grief associated with any loss. She may even be aggrieved if the child apparently does not mourn at all for the life that has ended. It is odd that it is so rarely recognized that for the child the real wrench may come at the other end of school life, when he is thrown out of the familiar world of school into the hard work-day world of the factory or the office and knows that this is a point of no return.

At the other end of the scale we are beginning to understand something of what the experience of retirement means. It is significant that the mortality of men is high in the years immediately following retirement. It is as if they are unable to survive the traumatic experience of leaving a way of life that may have been theirs for fifty years, and the unaccepted inner death becomes outer physical death. One of the reasons for the longer life of women may be that fewer women retire, since the work of the house and family must go on, and so even for the working woman there can never be a complete break with life, as the familiar household chores remain even when the job has finished. Preparation for retirement is beginning to be seen as vital, and it is not merely a practical problem of how to fill in one's time but a problem of adjusting to yet another death. From the psychological point of view enforced retirement is probably a harmful thing, however necessary it may be from an economic point of view. It is not always realized how vital a shock it can be to a person when work ends, or how enriching it can be for even very old people to continue in the working way of life. I remember an eighty-one-year-old lady fretting when a broken leg made a stay in hospital necessary. On inquiring I found that she ran a corner shop and got up every morning at 5.30 to go to market. She could not wait to get back to her shop and dreaded that once she was in hospital we would try and 'put her in a home', simply because she was old. She told me that she would die if she were condemned to sitting in an armchair looking at the four walls of a room, and she was probably right. In spite of the protests of a loving daughter who wanted her to retire, I sent her back to her shop and her early morning jaunts to the market, sure that she would die if forced to give up her way of life before she felt ready to do so. Another seventy-nine-year-old tried to discharge herself from hospital a few days after her admission with a fractured pelvis. She agreed to stay another week but no more. On inquiry I found that she was still working, in the tailoring trade, with the same firm she had worked with for forty-three years, and had no intention of retiring yet.

This point of readiness is of tremendous importance. If a person is prepared for a crisis or is equipped to deal with the emotions involved, then he is not overwhelmed by it. The caseworker's job is to see what is happening and recognize the symptoms when the death crisis is causing unmanageable grief and suffering. The difficulties occur when the crisis is not recognized for what it is, and either unsuitable remedies, or none, are offered. This can happen in adolescence. The onset of puberty signals the death of childhood, but this is too rarely understood by parents, teachers or others who deal with children. Adolescence can be an exciting time and most young people look forward to it with curiosity and excitement, but the many mood swings and especially the depression that can alternate with the excitement are just as characteristic and necessary a part of this stage of life. Childhood has to die and therefore has to be mourned, and the modern cult of the teenager may allow little time for this. Parents, even while they lament that 'they are not children long these days', may in fact push the adolescent into an adult way of life before he has had time to bury his childhood decently, and have a reasonable period of mourning. A regression to childhood may follow if this situation persists. Margaret Mead has shown that adolescence is not necessarily a time of stress, but is only so in societies that do not allow it to have its true significance. In some primitive societies where initiation ceremonies were held, when childhood could be seen to die and could therefore be properly mourned, there was no conflict in adolescence and it was a time of smooth development very different from the upheavals common in western society.

A similar situation can arise for a woman in the menopause. She may be heartily glad to be finished with the risk of further pregnancies and may enter into her married life with fresh zest. In practice, however, it often coincides with the children leaving home either for marriage or careers, and it may signify a real death to the woman who sees one aspect of her married life as finished. The depression that sometimes accompanies the menopause has one of its roots in the death of a phase of life that can never be lived again. The single woman may be mourning her unfulfilled motherhood, for even if she marries now, she cannot have her own children.

For some people there are other crises that mean a sudden end to the way of life they have known. Many events could be included in this category: marriage, emigration, the loss of virginity, the taking up of a new career during adult life, among others. Some of these are reversible and being self-chosen do not always have the inevitable feel of death. The onset of an incurable illness, as for instance arthritis, can mean the end of 'normal life' as most people know it, and from this there can be no turning back. The physical education of a diabetic, a polio victim or a case of heart failure needs to be supplemented by help in understanding and expressing the grief that naturally attends the death of a way of life. It may be expressed as anger and rage, 'Why should this happen to me?', or as rebellion and a refusal to keep to a diet by a diabetic, or rejection of a routine by a heart patient. In their anxiety to point out how much of life is left and to look on the bright side, relatives often refuse to allow the patient the time to mourn the death of the old life.

The other common situation in which a person experiences a sense of death is when for any reason work becomes impossible. Since the industrial revolution, our society has become so completely based on a principle of work that to be unable to work can be a very painful death. It is the real crisis of any major wave of unemployment. The dole may relieve the suffering of the families but it does not ease the crisis of the breadwinner, who has in a sense died to the working world and is excluded from the life to which he feels he belongs. Serious accident or crippling illness can have the same effect. Respiratory cripples suffering from chronic bronchitis can die of sheer hopelessness, because there seems nothing left to live for once they are excluded from the normal working world. The all too common break-up of marriage and family life that follows a man's incapacity to earn his living only stresses the fact that he is a ghost, with no significance in the living world.

These changes are for the most part not only inevitable but permanent. To some degree, however, there is a sense of death in any situation that entails a loss of freedom. The obvious example is that of prison, and however much it may be true that the old lag commits crimes in order to get himself safely back inside, to most people the loss of freedom is a real crisis. The recent examples of journalists released from house arrest in China illustrate how deeply people suffer from loss of freedom, even if they are confined in their own house and not in a prison cell. The efficient routine of a hospital rarely takes into account how much some people may suffer from the loss of freedom that hospital admission entails. Patients tend to be considered good patients if they die to their freedom quietly and are thought difficult if they resent the enforced discipline and the routine which seem designed for the convenience of the staff rather than for the comfort of the patient. A good deal of friction could be avoided if this were understood, and the patient could be helped through the crisis. Any serious illness can entail lack of freedom, especially an illness like TB that imposes a number of restrictions on the patient which, though they may not be permanent, seem to him to last a long time. Where the disability is permanent some degree of loss of freedom will be permanent also.

Perhaps the most pathetic loss of freedom is that experienced by those who have to leave their own home and go into a Home, which however skilfully disguised, is an institution. The young are often fortunate in having a social worker who understands them at this crisis, but it is not always recognized that old people can suffer in precisely the same way. Too often they are reproached for not settling down at once, when the old back-to-back terrace house, with a kitchen in the cellar, no bath or hot water and a toilet up the street is exchanged for the modern purpose-built welfare hostel. Life may be immeasurably better in the hostel, but it is not the life they know. The miserable house may have been home for fifty years, bought as a result of hard saving and thrift on the part of the young bride and bridegroom. To the old lady sitting silently and perhaps sulkily in the corner it may mean the end of her marriage, more final even than the death of her husband a few years previously, for now there is nothing but her wedding ring to symbolize the old life.

Any loss can in fact be an experience of death. This is an important element in the understanding of anyone who has to have a part of the body removed by operation, or which is lost by accident. The removal of an eye, for instance, from a medical point of view can be a relatively simple operation. From the point of view of the patient's feelings, however, it can be a major tragedy. It is not only the rational fear he may have that he may lose the other eye and so become totally blind. It is much more a deep sense of loss, that a part of him has been lost in the irrevocable way that someone is lost by death. This is even more obvious when a limb is amputated. Surgeons recognize the fact that there is more to it than a simple operation when they talk of 'phantom' limb pains. The patient may for some time feel quite severe pain in the limb that is no longer there. As the adjustment is made and the loss is accepted, the phantom limb will disappear and the pains with it. This is another example of the outworking of grief and mourning for what has been lost.

In the very different situation of marriage counselling it needs to be remembered that the loss of a partner needs to be mourned, whether the loss is caused by death or any other agent. In fact the less respectable loss by desertion will sometimes call forth a greater grief. The neighbours will often rally round with comfort and sympathy when a partner has a coronary or dies of cancer. This understanding may be lacking if a wife deserts or a husband commits adultery. A divorce is less respectable than a funeral, but it breaks the marriage even more effectively. It not only removes the partner physically but shatters the image as well, so that even the good memories of the past become questionable. Divorce, desertion or separation in a marriage cause a crisis, in which both partners, whether labelled the innocent or the guilty party, are in need of support for the loss they undergo.

A child may lose a parent in more ways than by physical

death. Child-care officers realize that when they take a child into care he is losing his parents in what to him is a very real sense. They may have neglected him, beaten him, utterly rejected him, but he still mourns them, and this must be taken into account by those receiving him into care. Most children are adopted at too young an age to experience this as a situation of loss, but adopting parents have to realize that the day may come when the child will have to mourn his parents. Even if he is told of his adoption, as he should be, at a very early age and accepts it happily and naturally, there may come a time when he realizes that he has lost parents as well as gained a home. To deny him his grief for this, and reproach him for ingratitude may turn his grief to aggression and rebellion in adolescence. The other side of the picture is easier to understand, and the mother who parts with her baby because she is unmarried and unable to care for him is usually treated more sympathetically and allowed her mourning. Even here the well-meaning family may urge her to forget, to put it all behind her and go out and enjoy herself, and they may be impatient if she can not do this at once.

This situation illustrates the dual nature of most crises: they involve not only death but birth. An old way of life dies, but a new way of life is born, and casework is concerned with the bringing to birth of this new life, and the fostering of it in every way possible. The mother of an illegitimate child has a life before her, which may well include marriage and other children. Just as she must be allowed to mourn, so she must not be allowed to stay at this point of death, but must be helped to go forward into a new life and new experiences.

One of the attractions of probation work is that it contains the possibility at least of never-ending experiences of new life. If some forms of casework seem to be geared to deal with the death crisis, probation ideally has its emphasis on the birth crisis. Its very philosophy of the second chance entails the acceptance of the idea of the possibility of new

73

life coming into being. The first offender may, because of the experience of probation, never commit another offence. Sometimes the old offender can surprise everyone by responding to probation and by showing evidence of the birth of new life in a way no one would have thought possible. The probation officer can only undertake his job if he believes in the possibility of birth, over and over again. Offenders lapse time after time, often with a dreary repetition of the same offence, but as long as they are put on probation, someone is believing in the possibility of new things coming to birth.

One could not work in a hospital setting unless one believed most firmly in the possibilities of birth at any time and at any age. There is a new birth whenever a patient gets up and starts walking again, an experience which can make the orthopaedic ward very satisfying. It may take months but whenever a patient is rehabilitated and sent back to his own home there is a sense of new life coming to birth. It is never quite the old life that is recovered nor the old person who goes back to it.

In mental illness there can be a similar experience of new life when a patient recovers. The recovery can often seem to be sudden and dramatic, and this enhances the impression of a new lease of life. I have known a patient so sunk in depression that when I said every week that it would lift, she could only shake her head wearily, and say, 'I shall never go back home. I shall never live with my husband and children again.' After many weeks of this I went in one day and found her striding across the ward, her hands outstretched to me and her face smiling with joy as she cried, 'It's happened just as you said it would. It's gone and I'm better.' It may sometimes take not weeks or months but even years, but birth is still possible and new life can spring up however long it is hidden.

The most dramatic evidence of new life that I have encountered was in a displaced person, who was taken to hospital with a broken leg. On admission she looked as if she had come straight from a concentration camp. She was dirty and verminous and so emaciated she might have been in the last stages of cancer. She spoke little English and was terrified of everything and everybody. She refused to sign the consent form for an anaesthetic to set her leg, and any attempt to try and make her talk either met with the response that she did not understand or that she was too tired. When she came to our hospital she had been cleaned up but otherwise she was a pitiable sight. She was referred to me as a Polish lady who had lived with her sister who was now very ill in hospital. I called in an interpreter, who established the fact that she was Ukrainian and had lived with her aunt. At first she would not speak to him and begged him to go away as she was too tired. Gradually he won her confidence, and she sat up and talked to him. We gave her warm clothes, although it was summer, for she complained bitterly of the cold. From our clothing store, we begged a pretty pink shawl which was intended for old ladies' shoulders, and which she used to put over her head, peasant fashion. She was taken to the shops and with great difficulty a pair of shoes was found for her, that did not hurt her feet, tender from not wearing shoes for so long. One day a nurse manicured her hands, washed and set her hair and gave her some make-up. She laughed self-consciously and said, 'I look like a monkey', but the amazing fact was that she at last looked ordinary. She was transferred to the rehabilitation ward and after her initial fears were calmed she settled down, ceased to wear her shawl, and no visitor would have noticed her except for her broken English. The welfare officer who knew her well did not recognize her when she came to visit. A new person, who had always been there in embryo, had developed. Although she was irreparably damaged in both body and mind, yet she had undergone new experiences that had opened up endless possibilities.

In some situations the death and birth crisis are both

present. An unmarried girl who becomes pregnant will at first seem to be entirely in the situation of one facing death. She sees the end of her life of carefree independence, and her reaction may be to desire death in some form. It may be the death of the child she desires, and she comes to ask to be referred for an abortion. In very many cases this will be refused and her reaction to this may be either a threatened or an attempted suicide. When she has been helped through this stage she may be able to see the other side of the experience and begin to accept the fact that it is not only an end to her old life but the beginning of a new life. Whether she keeps the baby or has it adopted she is unlikely to forget the experience of new life, however off-hand and casual she may appear outwardly. Penny, for instance, had a broken marriage that had resulted in divorce and a broken liaison behind her and the certainty of any number of relationships before her. The two children of her marriage were taken into care when she was admitted to hospital, so she was referred to the social worker. One day she was unusually quiet and thoughtful and explained it was her little girl's birthday. She said she would be five and then added that she had had her adopted because she was the child of a liaison she had formed when her marriage first broke up. She had never revealed before that she had had three children, but it was not because she had forgotten. No one could claim that Penny had become a new person with this experience but something had been added to her and it had not left her unchanged.

It may seem that the other meaning of crisis, that of decision, has little bearing on casework. In one sense we are always alone at the moment of decision. We may take advice, listen to opinions, but unless we make it ourselves it is not a decision but obedience to an order. Corporate decisions in a democratic society are only collections of individual decisions, each person making up his own mind, either in agreement or disagreement with the majority. The possible exception to this is the Quaker method of making decisions in which the chairman does not count votes but takes the sense of the meeting. It is difficult to assess what happens here. In practice many decisions will be made in the usual democratic way, but sometimes it may well be that in the end a group decision is formed out of the group concern.

In fact, however much social workers may protest that their principle is to allow the client to make his own decision, the act of decision-making is usually where help is most needed. There are few decisions which can be made in complete isolation. Even suicide, which is apparently the loneliest of all decisions, is usually made with reference to other people. It is not only that suicide often arises out of an involvement with other people, in a quarrel for instance, but the act itself is usually intended to influence other people. Mark Twain's account of Tom Sawyer's supposed death and his hidden presence at his own funeral service is a brilliant account of what most suicides really want: to hear other people admitting they have not appreciated him and to hear their regret for not having realized his value in time. The decision to attempt suicide has, in many cases, contained a cry for help, or a desire 'to show them'.

Decision is essentially the confrontation of two people: the one who makes the decision and the other who is affected by it. Casework is involved in the preparation for decision and in the consequences of it. There are times when decisions have to be made for people, but the caseworker has to prepare for the moment when this is not necessary and the person can accept responsibility for his own acts. Preparation for decision can take up the greater part of a caseworker's time. It may be that the person needs facts, accurate information, given in an unbiased way, before the decision can be taken. He may merely need someone to listen while his own mind becomes clear, as he talks over the issues involved. It may be that the caseworker acts as a guinea pig on whom the decision is tried out before the real action is taken. It may be a matter of support: the client knows quite well what he intends to do, but needs help to carry it out, either practical help, or merely the knowledge that someone else knows and approves the decision.

On the other hand, the caseworker may be needed after the decision has been taken. Again the help may be practical; help with rehousing, application to a welfare department, referral to other agencies; or it may be support to stand by the decision and help to face the consequences. The decision to allow a surgeon to perform an operation, to give up one's home, to accept the offer of rehousing, to give up one's baby for adoption or to adopt another woman's child, are all decisions that may require help long after they have been made.

To say, therefore, that casework is involved in crisis situations is not to imply that it is concerned only with a moment of drama and suspense. It is a work of preparation, involvement and support before, during and after decision. It is a dangerous occupation; the caseworker is always at risk, either of taking the easy way out and making the decision himself, or aiding and abetting the client to avoid making any decision at all.

6 The Method of Casework: (i) Listening

The key activity of a casework ministry is listening. Unless one is able to listen there is no point in undertaking casework training. It is the very antithesis of that ministry which is impelled above all to talk, which knows the answers without any questions needing to be asked. The casework ministry is not for those who feel that people need to be instructed and guided by one with a wisdom and knowledge superior to their own.

The best description of a caseworker is to be found in Jung's *Modern Man in Search of a Soul*.[1] Jung is describing the role of the doctor but the account fits the caseworker exactly. He calls the doctor's attitude 'unprejudiced objectivity', which he defines as a 'deep respect for facts and events and for the person who suffers from them – a respect for the secrets of such a human life'. He goes on to say that 'the truly religious person has this attitude. He knows that God has brought all sorts of strange and inconceivable things to pass, and seeks in the most curious ways to enter a man's heart. He therefore senses in everything the unseen presence of the divine will.' This acceptance of another person with reverence and respect is only achieved by discipline, which involves not only training in the formal sense but willingness to submit to self-discipline, so that one's inmost thoughts and feelings can be brought into the open and measured against this standard of unprejudiced objectivity.

The casework training in listening is not for a passive role of simply being present at another person's outpourings.

79

The listener's role is an active one and is based on certain specific principles. Most casework theory accepts Father Biestek's[2] seven principles as the essential ingredients of casework. The listener has at the outset to make a conscious effort to train himself on these lines and some students rebel at first, objecting to what seems to them a falsely self-conscious attitude. It is only later, when they realize that some of their unconscious attitudes may be unhelpful and even harmful to the other person that they are trying to help, that they accept the idea of training in listening attitudes.

The most important first principle is that of seeing each person as a unique individual. Any tendency to see people in categories or label them in any way is detrimental to real listening. It is easy to recognize 'types', and much more difficult to discern the individual beneath the type. It is not merely that one is tempted to label according to the setting one is in, and in hospital to classify people as amputees, paraplegics, chronic bronchitics, or in the probation service as shop-lifters, absconders, recidivists or wife-beaters, but there are subtler temptations to divide people into good and bad, sane and mad, helpful and difficult. Jung's unprejudiced objectivity demands that one sees each person as an individual who has become himself by a unique process, and as such is worthy of attention. Simone Weil in *Waiting on God*[3] defines love of our neighbour as 'creative attention'. She points out that difficult as it is to listen to someone in trouble it is just as difficult for him to know that someone is listening to him with compassion. To convince him that he is being listened to as he really is, that for the moment he and no other exists for the listener, is the first tremendous task of the caseworker.

It may seem to the beginner that it is in fact a very simple thing and may be achieved with very little trouble. During training the students' eyes are opened to the fact that this is achieved only with difficulty and at some cost. Two very different writers point out some of the difficulties. Harry

Stack Sullivan, an American psychologist, writing about the technique of interviewing,[4] reminds the interviewer that the first important fact is that the other person is a stranger to him. Many people acquire a technique of interviewing that always assumes an attitude of intimacy from the first moment. This is supposed to put people at their ease; in fact it may sometimes repel them, as it assumes that they are not individuals but that the interviewer, having seen one person, has seen them all, and so can immediately be on intimate terms with anyone. Remembering that he is a stranger makes it impossible to use the familiarities that are sometimes taken for granted in a geriatric ward, where everyone is Gran simply because they are old, and no one is allowed the courtesy title of 'Mrs'.

Sullivan points out that the other side of this is that the interviewer needs to know what impression he makes on strangers. Most of us are unaware of how our mannerisms, facial expressions and tone of voice affect other people when they meet us for the first time. The first painful lesson of the would-be listener is to see himself in the mirror of other people. At first this may mean a certain amount of self-conscious reflection and watchfulness, but once this initial stage is over there is a release and freedom that comes from knowledge and acceptance of one's own limitations. Sullivan does not suggest one acquires a perfect interviewer's manner, but that one becomes aware of what one is doing, and how the other person will be likely to react at the first encounter.

Douglas V. Steere writes in a very different way about the difficulties of listening in his Swarthmore Lecture *Where Words Come From*.[5] In an attempt to describe these difficulties he postulates the presence of a spectator-listener, who is within the speaker and listens while he speaks. This spectator-listener is a kind of radar that picks up at all levels what is going on. He is therefore able to gauge when the listener is not really listening, but merely appearing to attend. He is able to detect the reaction of the listener, his disapproval, disgust or rejection, his impatience or his boredom. 'What is going on in the outward listener's conscious mind, as well as what is occurring in the outward listener's unconscious, is never fully veiled to the speaker's inward spectator-listener.'[6] Douglas Steere points out that real listening is very rare for this reason and even the experienced listener needs to remind himself of this every time he prepares to listen to another person.

Once the interview has begun the listener has to learn to deal with and even encourage the expression of feelings. At first this can be a frightening experience and the listener tends to do all in his power to prevent feelings being expressed. Hasty reassurances, false comfort or even the abrupt termination of the interview will serve to prevent an outcry of grief or a burst of anger. Yet listening will be of no real value until a display of feeling can be tolerated and its purpose understood and used in the situation. The first instinct is to shy off the situation, to cover it up and pretend the emotion is not there, but if this is done no real listening will be possible. It must be possible for a person to confess whatever he feels, even if it is that he wants to end it all, because the pain or the worry or the frustration at that moment are more than he can bear.

In the case of Mrs B. it was not until she was able to show emotion that I had any clue to the complex nature of her problems. She came into our hospital with a serious disease of the spine having already been in two other hospitals for more than a year. She hoped eventually to make her home with her daughter, her only surviving relative, since her husband and son had died in the last few years of coronary thrombosis. One morning early a message came that her daughter had collapsed and died of a coronary thrombosis. She remained very composed and controlled and told me her son-in-law would be willing to have her in his home. It was some weeks later that I received an urgent summons to go and see her. The nurse had been bathing her when she began to cry bitterly. I thought it was her natural grief finding expression at last and so I made no attempt to talk but let her cry. When she spoke it was unexpectedly to say she wished she could go out of hospital so that she could see her solicitor. I was surprised but I told her there was no difficulty in arranging for him to come to hospital if that was what she wished. I phoned the number she gave me and within an hour or so a solicitor came out. He asked to see me after he had talked to Mrs B., and said he was appalled to hear of our intention to discharge her to her son-in-law. He could not tell me why, as the story was confidential, but he asked me to take his word that it was a seriously mistaken plan. If I would trust him on this point he would do everything he could to make it possible for her to return to live alone in her own home. I agreed and he was better than his word, as no son could have worked and planned more lovingly than he did to get Mrs B. home. That moment of emotion was the turning point in her problem. Had it been ignored or had she not been able to say what she really felt, a seriously wrong decision would have been made. Only the knowledge that I was really listening to her enabled her to bring out this deep trouble that was on her mind.

The most complex problem for a listener is that of involvement. Detachment can be made to sound scientific and it can be argued that it is useless to become too involved. The confusion arises because involvement is not clearly understood. It must be accepted that no one can listen without being prepared to become involved. The listener who is not vulnerable is not listening at any depth. Biestek talks about 'controlled emotional involvement'. Perhaps a more helpful description is conscious involvement. The harmful situation is the one in which the listener is unaware of his own reactions, so that the other person may deliberately arouse and use his emotional response. This unawareness may well cloud the listener's judgment and in the end will prevent true sympathy or feeling with the other. To be able to share the experience of the other, not confusing one's own emotional reactions with sympathetic feeling in a situation, is the aim of the listener. The fact that one is aware of one's own emotional responses does not mean that one rejects them; on the contrary the aim is to turn the feelings to good use in the helping situation. For instance a young girl with TB who is very frightened of the disease, who is a stranger to the country and who has recently lost her mother, whom she has nursed for many years, will look for a mother-figure in the social worker. To be aware of this is neither to run away from it, nor to let the situation control the listener, but to use it to help the girl to overcome her fear, accept her treatment and begin to plan for the future. One has to accept that for the moment she needs a mother-figure to help her through her illness. On the other hand one has also to be aware of the danger of one's own maternal feelings becoming uppermost, so that their satisfaction becomes the most important factor in the situation and not the girl's recovery. It is not an easy or a quick lesson, to learn to hold the balance between a rigid detachment on the one hand and an uncontrolled involvement on the other. Somewhere between these two lies compassion, which is the name Simone Weil gave to our attention to those in affliction.

Jung says of his doctor that if he wishes to help a human being he must be able to accept him as he is. No amount of sympathy or charity is a substitute for this. The success or failure of the listening depends on acceptance. Jung also points out that acceptance of another is only possible when we have accepted ourselves. This may sound very simple, but in fact it is a state of grace not acquired by a few simple rules. According to Jung 'acceptance of oneself is the essence of the moral problem and the epitome of a whole outlook upon life'.[7] It is in fact a recurring point. Acceptance of others depends on acceptance of ourselves, and self-acceptance only comes from being accepted. Tillich makes this clear in his sermon 'You are Accepted' in *The Shaking of the Founda-*

tions.[8] He suggests that sin, as a word, has no meaning in our time, but separation or estrangement does have meaning and that the experience of forgiveness in this age is the experience of acceptance. It comes to us perhaps in our darkest moment when life seems meaningless and empty, as if a voice were saying: You are accepted now, just as you are. In that experience Tillich believes there is a bridge across the gulf of estrangement, and we are reconciled to ourselves, to other people and to the world. He says:

> We experience the grace of understanding each other's words . . . We experience the grace of being able to accept the life of another, even if it be hostile or harmful to us . . . We experience moments in which we accept ourselves, because we feel that we have been accepted by that which is greater than we . . . We cannot force ourselves to accept ourselves. We cannot compel anyone to accept himself.[9]

Jung makes the point that it is impossible to accept the worst in another, unless we accept the worst in ourselves also. In one of his finest passages he emphasizes how difficult it is, especially for the virtuous, to accept themselves as they really are.

> That I feed the hungry, that I forgive an insult, that I love my enemy in the name of Christ – all these are undoubtedly great virtues. What I do unto the least of my brethren, that I do unto Christ. But what if I should discover that the least amongst them all, the poorest of all the beggars, the most impudent of all the offenders, the very enemy himself – that these are within me and that I myself stand in need of the alms of my own kindness – that I myself am the enemy who must be loved – what then? As a rule, the Christian's attitude is then reversed; there is no longer any question of love or long suffering; we say to the brother within us, 'Raca' and condemn and rage against ourselves. We hide it from the world; we refuse to admit even having met this least among the lowly in ourselves. Had it been God himself who drew near to us in this despicable form, we should have denied him a thousand times before a single cock had crowed.[10]

Even the psychotherapist finds it hard to accept himself in all his wretchedness and prefers to busy himself with other people and their problems. No one, Jung points out, can boast that he has fully accepted himself, but unless he has some idea of what this means he will never, in his listening, come close to the lives of other people.

Closely connected with this acceptance is the non-judgmental attitude of the listener. This is the most puzzling of the casework principles to the student, who either thinks he must agree with the other person at every point and ship overboard his own standards and values, or he believes the caseworker to be a hypocrite, pretending to agree with other people, while secretly sitting in judgment on them. There are those who say that nowadays sin is out of fashion and all actions are condoned. This is the ignorance of those who have never entered into an understanding of the depths of human nature, either in themselves or in others. To understand is not to condone, though it should be to forgive. Jung emphasizes that we cannot change anything until we accept it. 'Condemnation does not liberate, it oppresses. I am the oppressor of the person I condemn, not his friend and fellow-sufferer.'[11] Biestek's phrase 'non-judgmental attitude' is perhaps misleading, for the danger is not in judgment but in condemnation. Judgment we all have, and our standard of values is a vital part of ourselves. The purpose of casework training is to help us to sift values from prejudices, and to come to some understanding of the purpose of the gospel saying, 'Judge not that ye be not judged.' We all have our own areas of non-acceptance, where we condemn instead of understanding; one may have a deep understanding of prostitutes but be intolerant of alcoholics; another may enter into the problems of teenagers but have no patience with recidivists. It is not easy to listen to the person before you when she has beaten and starved her child, and the temptation is to see the victim as a person and to label the offender in a way that condemns and depersonalizes her. To feel the enormity of the suffering of the child and yet to be able to see the mother as a person also, and understand the events that have made her what she is, is what is required of the listener, if he is to be any use in the situation.

There must be no doubt in the mind of the listener that the ultimate end of the process is not the dependence of the other on him but a greater measure of independence. As far as possible he must make his own decisions and help must be directed towards this end. There are obvious limits to this; in extreme illness or insanity decisions must be taken on behalf of others, but it is all too easy to assume responsibility for those who could and should be responsible for themselves. People often want to shed responsibility and will ask 'What do you think I should do?', because it is easier to obey an order than to make a decision. Relatives sometimes openly say in disappointment that they hoped I would tell them what they ought to do for the patient, and I have to remind them that although advice, information and understanding are available, the responsibility for decision cannot be delegated. Sometimes the temptation to usurp this privilege is very great, as for instance when Mrs Y., on the housing list for a flat because she had had a leg amputated, refused the offer of a ground-floor flat. She could not accept that this was necessary and made the excuse that she would be nervous on the ground floor. If the social worker had said to her that she must accept she would probably have done so for she had become very attached to her. Yet she did not want the flat and said so emphatically, so the decision was accepted. Later she regretted the decision and a sympathetic housing manager made another offer, suggesting she should be taken to view the flat before deciding. This was done and she signed the contract the same afternoon. It was now her decision and she felt at ease about it, knowing she had accepted of her own free will.

When I was training for casework some social work tutors thought I would find this principle extremely difficult. They assumed that as a church worker I had acquired an authoritative role and had felt it my duty to tell people what they ought to do. Client self-determination was not thought to be a principle much used in the church, where we are supposed to presume to know all the answers, and to be only too ready to pass them on to others. I pointed out that in the story of the rich young ruler there is an excellent example of client self-determination which has always served me as a model. The respect shown by Jesus for the individual's decision, even when the person in question was completely mistaken, is one of his outstanding characteristics. It is unfortunate that too often we have not based our Christian ministry on this idea, but it is from the gospel conception of ministry that social work learned this principle. Both ministers and social workers may find it easier to be authoritarian, but real concern for people as individuals requires the listener to have the patience and the humility to accept the right of every person to make his own decisions.

Finally, the listener must be able to inspire trust and confidence in his integrity. The confidentiality of what is said must be assured. Sometimes this has to be said in words when the question is specifically asked. Experience teaches one to be wary before giving a rash promise. Some information must be passed on to others, if the person is to be helped. Once a hospital patient took out her glasses before signing a form, and I saw that she had tablets concealed in the spectacles case. I reported this to the sister-in-charge, feeling like a traitor, and knowing that the confidence between us might be destroyed. I knew also, however, that if she had taken an overdose in the night I should have been partly responsible. If patients confide symptoms but beg you not to tell anyone, then there is the very difficult situation in which they must be persuaded in their own interests to give permission for the information to be passed on. Alternatively, a confidence must be refused with the warning that it is better not to say things that the listener might feel bound to pass on. Legally any citizen must report crime which comes to his notice, and confidences of this nature can cause a good deal of worry to the listener. As far as casework records go, if a man tells me he has been in prison or a woman confides that she is not married to the man with whom she is living, and add that they do not wish anyone else to know, I simply forget to record the fact. It is there in my mind if the fact is needed but anyone reading the case record cannot stumble on the secret. For the rest, when a referral has to be made to someone else and information passed on, then usually a courteous request for permission usually meets with an acceptance of the situation and an acknowledgment that it is being done in order to help.

It is necessary, however, to realize that ideas of confidentiality are a cultural matter and depend very much on the social traditions and concepts of a person. Most English people expect private affairs to be treated confidentially and resent anyone else listening in. This is not true of other societies, and in dealing with Pakistani patients I have found confidence more important than confidentiality. Usually two or three of the more important members of the community, as well as an interpreter, will gather round for an interview. One man protested if anyone else came to listen, but he was the exception and for the most part casework interviews were treated like village councils. It seems as if justice must be seen to be done and I am always touched when everyone thanks me on behalf of the patient I have helped, as if it is truly a community concern. I have never insisted on seeing a Pakistani patient alone, as it seems to me false to impose on other people our purely local ideas of confidentiality. It seems to work, for they do not hesitate to send for me and have a touching confidence that I will solve all problems, however difficult.

The ministry of listening is a continual learning process. In casework training one grasps the abc and with constant practice one improves the basic skills, but the lesson is never completely learned. It is all too easy to break all the rules in a single interview and come away aware of a complete failure to establish any sort of relationship. The value of training makes itself felt here. It does not mean that one never fails in contact with people, but it should mean that it is possible to have at least some idea of why one has failed. Then, if a second interview is possible, the situation may be retrieved after all. If no second opportunity occurs, then at least one is forewarned against failure in a similar situation, or the case may be handed over to another worker who is better able to deal with it. In fact the whole ministry of listening might be summed up in the phrase 'to be aware'.

NOTES

1. Carl Gustav Jung, *Modern Man in Search of a Soul*, Routledge & Kegan Paul 1961, p.270.

2. F. P. Biestek, *The Casework Relationship*, Allen & Unwin, new ed. 1967.

3. Simone Weil, *Waiting on God*, Routledge & Kegan Paul 1951, p.90.

4. H. S. Sullivan, *Conceptions in Modern Psychiatry*, Tavistock Publications 1947.

5. Douglas Steere, *Where Words Come From*, Allen & Unwin 1955. Used by permission of the Friends' Home Service Committee.

6. *Ibid.*, p.7.

7. Jung, *op. cit.*, p.271.

8. Paul Tillich, *The Shaking of the Foundations*, Penguin Books 1962.

9. *Ibid.*, p.164.

10. Jung, *op. cit.*, pp. 271–2.

11. Jung, *op. cit.*, p.271.

7 The Method of Casework: (ii) Dialogue

Listening is so important that it is necessary to discuss it at some length, but it can give a mistaken impression. Casework ministry is not a one-sided affair at any point. If the idea of a minister doing all the talking and handing out the words of wisdom is false, then equally false is the picture of the silent caseworker who is the passive recipient of all that the speaker pours out in words and emotions. The illusion of the unmoved listener has indeed at times appeared in casework, modelled on what was thought to be the pattern of the psychotherapist, who was the silent recipient of the transferences of the patient. The analyst was presumed to have had all his responses analysed out of him, so that he was a mere sounding-board for the patient. This may be possible with a computer, but in a human being it is neither possible nor desirable. It is in fact the relationship, the two-way traffic, that constitutes the ministry and without this there cannot be said to be a casework ministry at all.

It is therefore misleading to describe the ministry as one of listening; it would be nearer the truth to call it a dialogue. The listener has to be willing to take an active part in the interview and contribute his share to the dialogue. If it is not easy to learn to listen it is even more difficult to learn to know the right moment to speak, and to be able to respond in a meaningful way to another person. The dialogue must further the situation in some way, either by establishing or confirming confidence, or by developing the solution to problems. To know when to encourage, when to be non-committal and when to offer positive suggestions, is only part of the art of dialogue. Words alone are not enough; the whole personality is involved and an essential part of the dialogue is the feeling on both sides. To be bored is an answer to a problem quite as effective as words of rebuke or condemnation. The art of dialogue is the ability to make a response in both words and feeling.

There are no exceptions to this rule of dialogue, even in situations in which at first sight it seems impossible. The most obvious hindrance to dialogue is the language bar. It is a mistake to think that the intervention of an interpreter will prevent the development of a relationship through which a person can be helped. It may well be the only way by which contact can be established, as it may be necessary for there to be some evidence that words are understood before problems can be presented with any confidence. It may also be that until a man can converse in his own language his real self does not appear. Mr K., for instance, was a Russian, a silent brooding man, who seemed sometimes to suffer from delusions, and who rarely answered with more than a monosyllable before relapsing into his dark silence again. One day it became necessary to make sure we understood each other. His sick benefit had by error been sent to his home address instead of to the hospital. The house was empty and as he never had any visitors, he had no prospect of getting the money. I could go and get the envelope but I needed the key and an assurance that the patient was willing for me to enter his house. The interpreter was sent for and came the next evening. He spoke a few words of Russian and the change was dramatic. The patient came alive and his face lit up, he laughed and words poured out of him in a joyful stream. I would not have known him. He was eager to co-operate and willingly produced the key and signed the authorization for me to enter his house. He talked happily for some time and the interpreter said afterwards that he was a very intelligent, well-educated man, who obviously had a very lively mind. After that, though Mr K. spoke no more English than before and I still spoke no Russian at all, there was more communication between us. I could never forget the animated person I had seen that evening and Mr K. obviously felt that some line of communication had been established between us and that I understood him as a person a little better than I had done.

It is an interesting experience to listen, for instance, to two Pakistanis in rapid speech with each other, and to watch for the expression on their faces and the movement of their hands, and then to have the position reversed and be watched in turn as the interpreter tries to convey what has been said. As the conversation goes backwards and forwards it is a dialogue, though a more remote one. It makes it clear that though words are important they are not the heart of the dialogue, which is something deeper, expressed also in feelings which are exchanged, but which goes beyond even feelings. In so far as it can be understood at all, it is probably what is described as relationship, the contact between two people which leaves neither intact, but alters, however slightly, the thought, the outlook and actions of both.

It is useful to have experienced dialogue under these conditions, so that one can gain some insight into how it may be used in spite of difficulties. I once had as a patient a Polish man who suffered under the Nazi occupation, and had finally escaped death only by a remarkable escape from a concentration camp. He refused offers to communicate with him in German and insisted that he spoke no German. He obviously thought in German and his English was very difficult to understand. He complained of headaches and other minor ailments, and the ward found him a bore, as he rambled on in incomprehensible English. One afternoon I had time to stop and listen to him. For nearly an hour I listened while he re-lived his experiences. Once I realized that he was thinking in German I could understand him quite easily and could follow him in his journey back into those feelings of fear and horror. There was nothing to be done in the practical sense after all those years, and I do not remember that I said anything beyond a few encouraging words from time to time. Yet at the end he said as I got up to go, 'Lady, one stone you have lifted from my heart.' More had been said than words and work had been done that could not be entered on a work study sheet, but could obviously be experienced.

It is helpful to be able to remember this when faced with the problem of communicating with those who have difficulty in this field. The deaf and dumb, for instance, are neither unintelligent nor unfeeling, and even without the finger language, dialogue is possible. Words can be written and expressions and gestures can convey feelings. Mrs M. was deaf and dumb, married to a man who was also deaf and dumb. She broke her leg and at the same time her husband developed a clot of blood on the brain which had to be removed by surgery. They were admitted to different hospitals about sixteen miles apart. Mrs M. could lip read and also used a pencil and pad for very brief communications. I had the responsibility of arranging when she was fit to go home and cope with the two of them. I felt it was necessary to have absolutely accurate information, so I called in an interpreter, in this instance the deaf welfare officer. Using the finger language he asked her all the usual questions about her home, and how she would manage her household duties with an injured leg. Then she began asking the questions, and the welfare officer explained to me that she was desperately worried in case the brain operation had affected her husband's mind. In vain he assured her that her husband had made a marvellous recovery and no one would know he had had an operation. She could not be convinced. Finally he asked if he would be allowed to take her to the other hospital to see her husband. I was sure this could be arranged, and after checking with the nurse in charge, asked him to tell Mrs M. it would be all right. No words were needed to know what she felt. She made the queer grunts that were the nearest she could get to speech, she nodded, clapped her hands and her eyes shone. I wrote 'Tuesday' in my notebook and showed it to her. She nodded again and settled back to wait. Some communication had been established on both sides. She knew that I understood her better in having seen some of her feeling for her husband, and I knew that she had correctly interpreted my immediate arranging of her visit to the other hospital as concern for her as a person, as distinct from concern about her broken leg. When the consultant on the ward round said she could go home, he muttered it into the case notes and I knew from one look at her face that she had not been able to lip read what he said. After the ward round I went back and wrote in my notebook 'Home Thursday'. Her response was almost overwhelming. She laughed and cried and jumped up and down in her chair, like a child. I went on to write in my book that I would ring the other hospital and arrange for her husband to be discharged on the same day. Then she was still; she sat and beamed and shone until I could feel the joy coming from her. I could not say, as I could to a hearing patient, how glad I was that she was going home, so I could only answer back in feeling, laugh with her, and truly feel happy about it, so that she could feel my joy as I felt hers.

The most difficult of all are those who have lost contact with reality; the psychotic and the senile. The most effective way of communicating with the psychotic is by persistent return to reality, to what is present and obvious to both. To unravel the tangle of fantasy is the expert's job and he may be able to communicate at that level, but for those without intensive psychiatric training dialogue must be at the reality level. When Mr W. tries to talk of his persecution complex, vaguely accusing 'them' of having radios to listen to his thoughts or of sending over planes to see what he is doing, and suspects the inoffensive young man in the next bed of being in league with 'them', nothing will be gained by trying to convince him of the unreality of his suspicions. Dialogue will only be possible outside these delusions. It will probably be necessary to listen to these first, but as soon as possible another topic can be introduced, closely related to concrete facts and tangible realities.

Senile patients present a different problem. On the one hand their confusional states can often show great variation. At one time they may be talking wildly and incoherently, and at another may be able to hold a perfectly sensible conversation, so that dialogue may be a matter of timing and patience, persisting until a clear moment is discovered. On the other hand the so-called ramblings of elderly people may be occasion for dialogue. In contrast to the psychotic, the elderly person's reality may truly be in the past. The present may have little to recommend itself and their talk is not fantasy, but fairly accurate remembering of the past. When Mrs D. calls me and with a very worried look asks me what she shall do because the woman over there has left a baby with her and she doesn't know if she is looking after it properly, and doesn't know when they will come and fetch it, I know that this is fantasy. I can only guess that either Mrs D. is jealous of the others in the ward who are getting my attention or she is truly worried about something but is too confused to know what it is. Either situation seems to be met by a few minutes beside her, a comforting touch on her hand and some reassuring words that she is doing very well, and not to worry, everything will turn out all right. When she asks anxiously, 'Do you think it will?' I can truthfully say yes to this, and after a few more minutes she seems satisfied and I can leave her. I could not say exactly what had passed between us but something had been communicated, if only anxiety and reassurance. The whole subject of the treatment of geriatrics is under discussion today, but one thing is clear, that if the old person is treated as a person in his own right, and not as an annoying or amusing child, he will respond with dignity and often with sense. I always address old people as Mr and Mrs, believing that if the personal dignity is preserved, much of the personality can be salvaged as well.

The ramblings of the old, however, can often be a means of communication. They are sometimes quite accurate memories, and if one has the time and patience, contact can be made by entering into these past experiences. A person may be thoroughly muddled about today's pension book but able to give a very clear account of farm life at the end of the nineteenth century. If one can accept the fact that this is how Mr R. sees himself, that he is still that farmer's boy, and at that point enter into discussion with him one may find later that it is possible to have a far more coherent conversation about the pension book. The time spent talking about the past has not been wasted, since it provides a foundation on which a present-day relationship can be built.

A student learning casework finds on the whole little difficulty accepting the idea of listening. Most students see the relevance of listening and are ready to learn not to rush in prematurely. More difficult to grasp is the concept of dialogue. One training device is the process report, a lengthy account of an interview, which is supposed to record not only the words used but the feelings displayed. Most students doing this for the first time manage, with some difficulty, to reproduce a verbatim account and some indication of the other person's moods and feelings. Their own responses, even their own words, may be almost entirely omitted, so that one is tempted to ask 'Where were you when this interview took place?' The reason is partly that the student is well aware that he is being trained and conceals his responses in case they are the wrong ones. This is not the only reason, for most of us are largely unaware of our own reactions. Our memory of an encounter may include 'He lost his temper', but not 'I was annoyed at his stupidity.' We feel other people's reactions when their words make them clear to us, but are often unconscious of what has provoked the reaction, or how we responded to it. It is this awareness that the casework student has to learn, so that the two-way process can be a real dialogue.

There was no doubt about the reaction of Mr A., for instance, when I first interviewed him. He had been listening outside the door while the charge nurse told me that Mr. A.'s wife had visited the day before and said he need not bother to come home as she had another man. When I opened the door I was confronted by a small man in a dressing-gown, his face bright red, his blue eyes glaring, a man so very angry he could hardly get out the words with which he demanded to know what I had been saying. To pretend that I had no reaction to this would either be a lie or an indication that I should not be doing social work. I could have been angry in reply; after all, he should not have been listening outside the door and he had no right to query my discussion with the charge nurse. I could have been frightened, for he was certainly in a fury. In fact my chief reaction was one of dismay; I felt appalled at the thought of trying to retrieve a situation that had begun so hopelessly. There seemed only one thing to do; to face it at its worst and see what could be made of it. I took him to the ward sitting-room, partly to give myself time to think, and partly to show him that I realized his need for privacy. Having told him exactly what had been told me, I handed it over to him and waited to see what he would do. His real feeling was his concern for his wife, and his fear was that I would so sympathize with him that I would refuse to help her. He felt helpless, frustrated by his illness that made him unable to fight back against the circumstances that had taken his wife from him. Perhaps what I felt at that moment mattered less than I thought at the time, and it was only important that I responded in a real way, accepting the situation and not only entering into dialogue but making it clear that I was doing so. I often saw Mr A. angry, sometimes with me if I failed to come at once when he sent for me, but he was angry as a child is, knowing that he is accepted and can have a fit of temper if he is off-colour or unhappy. Sometimes he was able to be angry with his wife and could show this too, no longer afraid that I would not understand that he could not help continuing to care for her. The dialogue with Mr A. lasted about eighteen months until he died suddenly one weekend. It had included concern for his delicate little girl in a special school, and correspondence with a soldier son in the Far East. He died, I believe, of a broken heart, but I also think that he struggled on sometimes because while someone was concerned with his problems they were not hopeless. He could not be cured, but some of his suffering was made more bearable.

This raises the vexed question of involvement. There is the school of thought which believes any form of involvement is anathema, and the opposite school for which detachment is a polite label for indifference. The difficulty with Biestek's neat phrase 'controlled emotional involvement' is that it does not explain how much control or how much involvement. Probably there is always a strong personal element in the dialogue situation, and the question of how much involvement will be decided by one's own temperament. When Mr A. died the Ward Sister rang me as soon as I arrived on the Monday morning, saying that she knew I would want to know at once that he had died. She obviously recognized a degree of involvement that went beyond a mere professional interest in a case. Each caseworker has to make his own decision. For my part I decided that, since one inevitably makes mistakes, I would make mine on the side of involvement. Believing that genuine caring in the end could not be harmful, I hoped that I would be able to increase my self-knowledge so that I should not confuse concern for others with self-indulgent emotions. The danger was that I would gratify my own need of having others dependent on me, and under the guise of feeling for others would fall a victim to the delusion of being the universal mother. Yet I believe this danger to be not so great as that of going by on the other side for fear of being involved in what might prove to be a difficult or painful situation.

On the other hand, it is important to accept the fact that no one person can be all things to all men. There are occasions when for one reason or another no real dialogue can be established. The reason may be quite simple and basic: temperamental incompatibility. Caseworkers are real people and their training should not have ironed all the individuality out of them, so that there may be occasions when they encounter a personality with whom they have no contact at all. It may be important for the caseworker to examine the situation and try to discover why there is this complete lack of dialogue, but from the client's point of view the answer is to find someone who can communicate. The ability to recognize one's limitation is a very necessary part of a caseworker's development, provided that it leads to the humility to hand over a case when necessary.

Mr J. presented just such a challenge. He was a Scotsman of about forty, brought into hospital following a serious road accident. He had severe brain damage, his speech was affected and one hand was useless. Both legs were broken and as far as we could discover he had no next of kin and no address. Communication was difficult, but we gradually pieced together odd bits of information; he had been in prison; he had had mental treatment; he had always been a social inadequate, rarely working, living in dosshouses or sleeping rough, and had probably been an alcoholic. He became alternately aggressive and depressed and suicidal. One day after an outburst the consultant tried to talk to him. He could give no reason for his anger, but that he never had any visitors. I felt guilty I had not realized this before and immediately set about trying to find a volunteer visitor. His language could be rather lurid at times so I could not ask anyone who would be easily shocked. I thought of the Quakers and their tradition of prison visiting. I had recently met a Friend at an inter-denominational group and I rang to ask him if anyone in the local Society had been a prison visitor. I explained what I wanted and he offered to come himself as he was a psychiatric social worker. He came and in the first few minutes achieved what I had been unable to do in many months: he entered into dialogue with Mr J. who immediately accepted him as a friend and began to watch eagerly for his visits. There may be many reasons why I was unable to speak to this man but the vital thing was to realize his need and find someone to answer it.

The fundamental need to communicate and enter into relationship is not necessarily a one-to-one experience. In the future, casework training will include more study of group work. There are situations in which communication is easier in a group than in a face-to-face encounter, and some people are more readily helped in this way. Group work is being used in probation, prisons, approved schools, mental hospitals and for parents of children suffering from a specific disability, either physical or mental. Some teacher-training courses include what is called group dynamics and many industrial or business concerns send key employees for training in group theory. The theories of what happens in a group are many and varied but the essential fact is that it is a means of communication and in certain circumstances can also be a means of healing. It is the basis of such movements as Alcoholics Anonymous, where support is given to each member, since all have been alcoholics and each feels he is accepted and understood. From this group support he draws strength to make the effort to recover his health and sobriety. In imitation of AA there are groups for gamblers, and the technique is also used in drug-addiction centres and, in one hospital at least, for psychopaths. That there is a ministry of groups has been accepted from the early days of the church. It has been assumed for too long that no special skill is required to exercise this ministry, and a study from those who have such experience in this would be a valuable addition to the current literature on the subject.

8 The Method of Casework: (iii) Attention to Detail

Caseworkers may be tempted to think that relationship can be achieved directly from person to person, without any intermediary. This is the lure of spiritual religion that has no need of the Incarnation, and believes it is possible to have the inner without the outer reality. Christianity insists that if man is not flesh alone, he is also not spirit in spite of flesh but a whole being. The goal of Christianity is this wholeness, which is more than health of body or mind and more than the salvation of a separate entity called the soul. It is a welding together of the separate elements of a man to make a whole person, in which body, mind and spirit work in harmony. In some religions this has been obtained by the subjection of the body and in others by indulgence of it. In Christianity neither is possible but both are replaced by a kind of teamwork which aims at the perfect development of the whole man.

The Church has by no means always preached this, for the negative religions have a fatal attraction for man, who finds it easier to deny those things he fears, than to accept and use them. It sounds loftier to insist that man is spiritual and that he can attain wholeness by nothing but spiritual means. The whole tenor of the gospel, however, is the insistence that man must dare to be a whole man if he is to inherit the kingdom. The very fact of the Incarnation makes it clear that God himself, when he wished to communicate with men, used neither purely spiritual nor intellectual means, but sent a man of flesh and blood who himself spoke to men through the medium of ordinary life.

The media of casework are the tools of service. Its badge could well be the towel and basin, though these symbolic tools would stand for a whole host of services in the welfare state. There is a tendency in some caseworkers to hanker after 'pure' casework, unmixed with any lesser elements of practical service. If this could be achieved, then it would cease to be casework. No one has purely emotional problems; people have problems of living and the deepest conflicts and perplexities make themselves felt in all the everyday concerns of life. The caseworker, therefore, needs the details of everyday problems of living as the medium through which he is going to achieve the relationship, which will bring about whatever measure of wholeness is possible at that point.

Most of us express our difficulties and conflicts in details. When we are worried or upset we slap the child, shout at the cat or find fault with our colleagues, usually rationalizing as we do so to justify our action. This is not to say these details are unimportant: quite the reverse. If we are attuned to attend to detail, then these situations are very revealing. People in hospital, for instance, are usually worried by some aspect of the situation. They may be worried about their illness and its outcome, about their future prospects, their home and family, about the routine of the ward, the behaviour or conditions of the other patients, or the attitude of one particular member of staff. Hospital and all the paraphernalia that goes with it arouses a good deal of anxiety, which makes it impossible for most people to express their feelings. Most feel at the mercy of the doctors and nurses and think that they must be 'good', or they will be made to suffer. They believe that they cannot ask questions, much less express criticism. Their anxiety may therefore be expressed in great fussiness about things outside the ward routine: sick benefit, rent or home help. The social worker may be seen as a 'safe' person on whom to vent their anxieties, because she is not closely linked either with the doctor and the medical diagnosis or with the nurses and the

103

routine of daily care. The patient may therefore become very demanding, continually wanting small services that she could perfectly well do for herself, or may ask for reassurance that has already been given many times. If the problem entails correspondence the patient may ask every day if an answer has been received. Another patient, having seen the social worker, may then tell his troubles to the physiotherapist, the nursing auxiliary, the occupational therapist and the porter, all of whom will faithfully report it to the social worker!

In these circumstances it is easy to become impatient and under the pressure of work brush off all these details as unimportant. The real answer is to ask why the patient needs to accumulate all these attentions. When the patient is Asiatic I believe that the answer is often cultural. I remember the widow in the parable who was heard not because of the justice of her cause but for her much importuning. When the social security has given a verdict that is not as favourable as was hoped for, I am often asked over and over again to inquire if more money will be granted. However much I explain that this is the law, and no other answer is possible, I still get asked the same hopeful question, and here I believe there is no point in looking for any worries or conflicts, it is simply a test of strength. The questioner believes that social security, like the judge in the parable, will get fed up in the end and yield to pressure.

There are other occasions when attention to detail in the literal sense is not what is required. One afternoon I was sent for to see a patient in a chronic chest ward. The nurse in charge was at his wits' end, as the patient was nearly beside himself with worry and the nurse could not make out the cause of it, in the brief moments he could spare to listen. At first the problem seemed real enough. The patient was a bachelor who lived with his sister. He was very worried because a visitor to the ward had referred to an accident reported in the evening paper. He was afraid it might have been his sister who was involved in the accident. If this were so he would not know about it as no one would realize he was in hospital. He went on to explain that if his sister were in hospital the house would be empty and thieves could break in and again he would not know. For some time I could not make out whether this had happened, or whether he was afraid it might happen, or if the fear had become fantasy and he thought it had happened. At times he seemed to realize that he was worrying about something that could happen but had not yet done so, and at others he seemed convinced that it was a fact. I listened for about three-quarters of an hour until I was sure that in fact nothing had happened. I inquired of the nurse in charge, who told me that his sister rang up every day and was certainly not in hospital. I suggested he should send for the doctor and ask him to prescribe a tranquillizer. I assured the nurse that to the best of my knowledge there was no problem that I could deal with, but that the patient was undoubtedly worrying and needed to be calmed. I never discovered what had been worrying the patient but to my surprise a few months after his discharge he sent me a cheque for the patients' fund, and has continued to do so every three or four months for the last few years. In this case the details in themselves were not important but attention to them was vital, in order to discover what the real need was; whether it was a phone call to the police about recent accidents or a call to the doctor for a prescription.

Very often, however, it is detailed knowledge that is required. It used to be assumed that each branch of social work needed its own body of specialized knowledge. It is now realized that in fact most social workers meet the same problems, whether the person in need is met in a hospital bed, a prison, a family service unit or a magistrate's court. All social workers need to know the working of the welfare state. In any setting one meets people with difficulties with social security allowances, sick benefit, family allowance, maternity grants and industrial benefit. Social administration can seem a very dry subject to the student who is longing to go out and do some casework, and it is not always easy to persuade the eager student that a sound grasp of the details of the welfare state is the foundation on which his casework will be built. Nor is it enough to know current legislation, or even that of the post-war years only. However young the caseworker may be he will have clients who remember the 'hungry thirties' and the indignities of the means test, and others who remember the Poor Law and the workhouse. These memories will colour their attitude to supplementary allowances and to welfare hostels for the elderly, as well as attempts to assess their income for services like home help. The details of past history must be grasped if these attitudes are to be understood and the person helped. I once had a patient who was a very forceful and aggressive person. She had bullied a surgeon into amputating her foot, and in the hospital ward she was bossy and outspoken with both staff and patients. She could not be understood without a knowledge of her background and some idea of what it meant. In the early years of the twentieth century she had been placed as a baby in a workhouse. That she had survived at all indicated a fighting nature. In these circumstances the weak and unresisting infants would not survive into adult life. When she left the workhouse she went into service and found that whenever her origin was revealed she was treated at best with contempt and at worst was actively ill-treated, it being assumed that anyone who came from a workhouse was of little account. Her aggressive manner was a habit, learned so long ago and so deeply that now she could not dispense with it, although the term workhouse has ceased to have any real significance at all for most people. When one knew both her history and its meaning one could understand her reaction to other people and to situations.

It is difficult for some young people who remember only the welfare state to understand the attitude of some older people to the social worker in hospital, who was once called the almoner. For instance, a letter to a certain patient's relatives brought in a nervous group who handed over to a bewildered social worker a rent book, pension book, statement of rates, electric bills, TV rental agreement and a host of other details of her financial affairs. The social worker had only wanted to discuss the discharge arrangements with them and was puzzled by this collection and even more by the relief on their faces when she disclaimed all interest in the patient's finances. The situation only became clear to her when I reminded her that before 1948 the almoner was often used in the hospital to assess the patient's financial situation and so decide how much he should contribute towards his treatment. I have had older patients who have become quite distressed when I have refused to take from them the money they offer for their maintenance in hospital. One old lady told me that she had made her son bring in to her a sum of money to pay me on the last day of her stay in hospital. When I refused it, she was indignant and said she knew people who had a pension handed it over, and though she had no pension, she did not want charity, but was quite ready to pay as everyone else did. I did not really convince her that hospital treatment is now free and I am afraid she left believing that I had assessed her as too poor to pay. The fact that the government reduces pensions after a person has been eight weeks in hospital is taken as proof that hospital treatment must still be paid for, and many relatives come to my office meekly handing over pension books, telling me that they know I will want them, as the patient now has to pay. Some knowledge of what the procedure used to be is necessary if these attitudes are to be understood. The details of social history may seem at first to be boring and irrelevant, but face to face with people who have lived through this history, its significance becomes clear. As tools of interpretation the details have obvious values.

It is not only detailed information that can be important,

but the apparently trivial words of the speaker can at times reveal the very clue the caseworker has been looking for. It may not be that the speaker is consciously hiding his real trouble or anxiety; he may himself be only half aware of what is wrong. His words, apparently carelessly chosen, may to the attentive ear suddenly reveal the problem that needs to be tackled. Unless one listens attentively the vital clue may easily be missed. When one is listening all day and every day, it is a great temptation to switch off and let the speaker ramble on, without really hearing the words that are spoken. In social work in hospital it may sometimes be the chance reference to an illness or a symptom, or to some previous treatment, that will throw light on an otherwise inexplicable feature of the patient's situation. It is incredible that sometimes patients can undergo treatment in several hospitals and pass through the hands of a number of doctors, nurses and social workers without certain vital facts being discovered. One patient, a psychopath, had experienced his eighteenth admission to a mental hospital before it was discovered that he had been through a bigamous form of marriage with his wife, and was tormented partly by his own conscience and fear of discovery, and partly by the fears of his wife, who had discovered the truth. Divorce proceedings were started and the police to whom he confessed the affair decided to take no action. It is astounding that this detail took so long to come to light. Some patients come to hospital with such a collection of past notes that it is difficult to find time to read them all. Yet sometimes half an hour spent reading these notes will reveal one detail that makes the whole problem look quite different. The irrational fear and deep depression of a patient whose broken leg or slipped disc is progressing well, may be explained when you realize that fifteen years ago she had an operation for cancer and now fears that it may be re-occurring. She needs reassurance that there is no connection between that former illness and her present accident, but was not even able to put her fear into words without help. A casual remark by the patient or a relative about another member of the family may explain some worry or fear that the patient has. Sometimes an apparently unimportant detail is thrown into the conversation to see if the caseworker will pick it up, and so open the way for a discussion of the real problem. One woman, when we were discussing how soon after her operation she could go home, mentioned casually that her husband worked all day in their own business and went out dancing every evening, so that she was alone all the time. This was the first clue she had given me that her marriage had difficulties. From there she was able to go on and discuss some of the problems of her home life. Later, another patient said how sorry she was for this woman who had endured so many years of an unhappy marriage, and it was obvious that the patient had talked to her neighbour in the next bed before she had thrown out a hint to me, to see if I would take it up.

One of the most important, yet often one of the most difficult details to which a caseworker must attend, is that of referral. It is inevitable, when the caseload is heavy, that sometimes there should be an interval before the referral is taken up. There is only so much time and some things have to wait while others are being dealt with. One can only choose one's priorities and hope they are the right ones. Sometimes they are not and then one is reminded all over again of the importance of attention to detail. On the orthopaedic ward I usually see each patient within a few days of admission, to discover the situation for discharging the patient. Sometimes pressure of work on other wards means a delay, and then I take a quick look at the admission book and try to assess from the basic details which patients are most likely to be in need of help, usually picking out those who live alone, are very old or have had a very serious accident. I can be very wrong. One morning I went to fetch a patient in order to take her to the hospital chapel for a communion service, and found her crying by her bed. She was an active middle-aged woman, did not live alone, and was making good progress. I had been very busy and a member of my staff was off sick, so I had decided to put off seeing her. That morning, therefore, I met her as a stranger and was not surprised when she would not tell me what was wrong. She said no one could do anything and there was no point in talking about it. I accepted defeat, knowing that if I had seen her when she was admitted she might have felt differently. I took her to the service and sat with her, and afterwards, when I came back later in the day, she did talk a little to me and explained the business worries she had concerning her late husband's affairs. It was true I could do nothing, but I could at least have known she was worried.

It is a continual temptation to want to brush aside details in order to achieve wholeness, but the fact is that wholeness is not achieved by sweeping generalizations or abstract theories. It is by attention to detail, by a loving understanding of the importance of detail, at a particular moment, in a particular situation, that a person is helped to become whole. Mother Julian of Norwich saw a hazel-nut as symbolizing all that is, and to be able to see the significance of an apparently trivial detail is to have the gift of insight.

9 The Goal of Casework: Making Whole

The aim of casework is to put together some of the disjointed parts of the personality so that, at the end of the process, the person emerges more whole than before. It recognizes that this is a lifelong process, and that the goal of human life is to make this wholeness as complete as possible. All experiences can contribute towards this, and for most people it never ends, for we never arrive at the goal of absolute wholeness, but are always capable of becoming more complete personalities. If salvation is the task of ministry, this is only another way of saying the same thing. Salvation, too, is a continuous process and we are always being saved from one state to another. Salvation is not a word that is meaningful to everyone today, when the psychologists talk about integration and maturation, but the process of being saved is familiar to anyone who deals with people in a crisis situation.

One of the most rewarding experiences is to see people saved from dependence into independence. Mrs K., after suffering a stroke, was seen at her home by a consultant who ordered her into hospital and told her while she was there to make up her mind to give up her flat and go into an old people's home. Her daughter, with the best of intentions, made inquiries at the home nearest to where she lived, although in fact her mother was not eligible for admission there. By the time Mrs K. was transferred to our hospital she was thoroughly depressed and hopeless about the situation. There did not seem any reason why she should give up her home, so I suggested to her that we worked at the problem from the other end; that we assumed that she could go home and tackled the difficulties as they occurred. At one point it seemed as if we would be defeated when she became very ill and had to be transferred to another hospital. However, she recovered and returned to us. Once more we began talking about the problems of going home and living on her own.

She had a flat in a modern tower block, and though she was a dozen stories up, there were lifts. She asked if we would take her home and assess her ability to manage, as we had done for another patient. This seemed a sensible suggestion, so the ward sister and I took her home one afternoon. We spent a very profitable afternoon, during which we found a hidden tea-trolley that would enable her to push her meals from the kitchen to the lounge, and tested fire switches and other appliances to make sure she could reach them. I made her move about the flat as if she were doing her daily chores, so that we could spot any difficulties. She managed very well indeed, and apart from aids in the bathroom little was needed to make it possible for her to manage. Shopping was the biggest problem as the blocks of flats did not include a shopping area. We suggested her family might do weekly shopping for her, and as she had a large family 'fridge, she would be able to manage with this. I also hoped that I might be able to find enough home help to ensure that the odd errand could be carried out when necessary. Once the welfare aids had been fitted there was nothing more to be done. She had spent some time on our rehabilitation ward, (nicknamed by the patients the 'do-it-yourself' ward) and so she had got into the way of doing household jobs like washing up, dusting and making cups of tea. It had taken some time to achieve this, but when we finally arranged her discharge it was with the knowledge that another patient had been saved, for at least a time, from the dependence and inactivity of a welfare home.

In most situations the salvation consists of a return to

what may be called a more normal way of living. The homeless patient, for instance, needs to be saved from this rootless situation. This presents a very difficult problem in my present appointment. The hospital is situated in very lovely country on a hillside overlooking a famous beauty spot. The patients I deal with mostly come from two large industrial cities, each about eighteen miles away. It is not easy to find accommodation from this distance. When a patient, usually a man, involved in a road accident, is entered in casualty as 'no fixed abode', most often this means he has neither friends nor relatives, and has probably lived casually for some time. In many cases I can only send them to the Salvation Army Hostel, where they can stay until they can find lodgings for themselves. The problem is altogether different when the patient is a woman. One of the cities has what used to be a common lodging house, but the consultant will not agree to women being sent there, although welfare officers assure me that the women's section is perfectly clean and respectable. Miss M. was one of the few women who had to be classified of 'no fixed abode'. She had worked in residential jobs all her life and when she was knocked down by a car and taken to hospital, she received a letter saying her post would be filled in her absence. The welfare department could only suggest the lodging house. It did not seem suitable for someone who had held posts of responsibility all her life, yet we could not keep her in hospital indefinitely. She was a Roman Catholic, so I appealed to her priest, assuring him that we would not discharge her until he found her a home. After a while he got her a room with the nuns, while he applied to a housing association for a flatlet for her. When she lost her job she had been very upset, and she seemed to be a very rootless and friendless person, probably because she had moved a good deal and always lived in institutions. She was delighted at the prospect of a home, and I have no doubt that she felt rescued from a very bleak homelessness into the security of belonging again.

One of the most moving examples of the salvation of a patient was that of Mr Z. He was a Pole who had been seriously injured in a road accident. He appeared to speak hardly any English and was very depressed. I asked the interpreter to come and see him and we were able to discover some of the things that were worrying him. The doctor had ordered an X-ray for the following week, and Mr Z. thought he was being ordered to go home within a week. He could not yet walk even with crutches. I was able to assure him, through the interpreter, that he would not be sent home until he could walk safely. When he was fit to go home the interpreter offered to take him in his car. It was the Saturday before Easter and we were rather worried about his lodgings. I had written to his landlady asking her to get supplies of food in, but I had had no reply. The interpreter took Mr Z. to the address he had given us. When he knocked at the door it was finally answered by the landlady who was dressed only in a nightgown and was obviously very drunk. The house was in a dreadful state and the hall had holes in it where the floorboards were missing. Mr Z. had already entered the house, but the interpreter quickly weighed up the situation and without a word he picked Mr Z. up in his arms, carried him out to his car, and drove off. He parked the car in a side street and soon discovered what none of us had suspected: Mr Z. had been an alcoholic, and the depression he had suffered on admission had obviously been part of his withdrawal symptoms. The interpreter asked where the nearest Polish shop was, and finding a little corner stores he went in and inquired if they knew of any clean, respectable lodgings. After some consultations they directed him to a nearby house. Leaving Mr Z. in the car, the interpreter went into the house and had a long talk with the landlord. He told him the whole story and asked him if he would take Mr Z. as a lodger, look after him, see that he had good food to eat and on no account buy him any drink. The man promised so the interpreter paid him a month's rent and brought Mr Z.

in to him, saying he would return in a week or two to see that all was well. As he told me this story the interpreter had no idea how much it sounded like the story of the Good Samaritan. He has returned several times to see Mr Z. and so far all is well. There is no guarantee that under stress or difficulty Mr Z. may not return to the comfort of alcohol, but for a time at least he has been saved from it, and like a twisted blackened tree, blasted by a storm, has put out a few shoots of new green life.

The ageing of the mind and the relapse into childishness and complete senile confusion is a distressing state to see. Sometimes it is possible to salvage the mind, when the confusion is due to shock, illness or accident. In an orthopaedic ward that receives patients from road accidents, one sees many apparently very confused people. Mrs E. was an old lady of nearly ninety. She had lived alone in a cottage in a village outside one of the big cities. She had several devoted nieces, who took it in turns to visit her, do her washing and help with the cleaning. Apart from being rather deaf she had no disabilities and was a delightful old lady, whom they all loved. When she came to us after her accident she was a strange, difficult person. When the consultant did a ward round she refused to get up out of her chair and walk for him, and when he tried to take her hand and help her up she clung to the chair and screamed at the top of her voice. She refused to speak to me, folding her lips firmly and giving me sidelong, suspicious looks. When her nieces visited her, she accused them of having sold her house and all her possessions, and defrauding her of her pension. I found one of them in tears in the corridor, saying she could not bear to come to visit her aunt again. I talked to her and tried to encourage her to go on hoping. If there had been no previous signs of senility, I told her, it might be due to shock and therefore might gradually diminish. She continued to visit her aunt and we went on gently trying to coax Mrs E. back to life. She learnt to walk, got used to the ward and the staff and gradually returned to her former personality. One day when I went into the ward she was busily writing letters and told me she really must get started on them as she had received so many while she was ill. Soon after that one of her nieces invited her to stay with her for a month's convalescence. She went, happily planning to return to her cottage at the end of the month.

Confusion cannot always be reversed and sometimes a patient is unable to return to her former way of life. Phoebe was an example of this. She was a fine, tall, upright woman, who looked much younger than her eighty years and could easily have been mistaken for a very vigorous seventy-year-old. She lived with an unmarried daughter who had a good professional job. When Phoebe's leg healed, her mind did not. She walked about the ward and the hospital grounds, was pleasant, cheerful and always had a sweet smile on her face, but had no clue where she was or what she was doing. She obviously could not be left alone all day so she had to be referred for welfare care, and spent many months waiting for a vacancy in the special psychiatric hostel. While she was with us we opened a new chapel for the patients, and the vicar began to take a weekly communion service on a Friday morning. I agreed to take patients from the orthopaedic ward and one morning the nurse on duty told me that Phoebe had suddenly told them that she was going to the service. She had heard it announced on the Tannoy system and was determined to go. She had been told that she could not, but I decided that I would take the risk and let her go with me. I took her hand and asked her to help me with the patient whom I was pushing in a wheelchair. Phoebe sat beside me, quiet and composed, her eyes shining with pleasure. After that I took her every week and she told me that her father had been a Methodist local preacher and as a child she had accompanied him to many different chapels. She loved music, and every week asked me if there was an organ in the chapel, as she loved to play the organ. Before

116

the service began she would talk to me quietly and sensibly, so that one day one of the young nursing cadets who had helped me bring the patients in that morning said to me afterwards in surprise, 'Phoebe was talking to you quite sensibly in the chapel.' One lovely autumn morning she sat staring out of the window at the sunshine and the trees that were a riot of colour, and finally she said softly, 'Aren't they beautiful?' Then she turned to me and said, 'I feel better when I see beautiful things, don't you?' I held her hand and a number of thoughts went through my mind. I thought angrily of the squalid institutions where some geriatric patients are kept, it being assumed that they hear nothing, see nothing, and smell nothing. Phoebe was incurably senile, yet beauty touched her and brought her to life again. We had not been able to make her whole again, but some life had been salvaged, and when music or autumn glory or the familiar words and actions of the communion service touched her, she sparked into life again.

There are some problems that have no obvious answer and it is not possible to see where wholeness can be achieved. Sometimes all that can be done is to release the person from some of his bonds and hope that in this freedom new life will begin to grow, as foxgloves grow in a cleared wood or rosebay willow-herb on a demolition site. Jock was just such a case. He was a strange, wild Scotsman who had been very badly injured in a road accident. His broad Scots speech was made more unintelligible by his injuries which had affected his brain and his speech, as well as leaving both legs broken and his left arm useless. He suffered badly from frustration at being unable to express himself, and especially at being confined to bed. Sometimes he went berserk, swore and raved and threw his crutches, his water jug or anything else at hand at anyone within reach. We thought at first he would be a hopeless cripple for the rest of his life, and wondered how he would face it. He had been a restless man, not very bright, always socially inadequate, only working when he needed money for food, living rough, sleeping in old buildings or at dosshouses. When, after a long time he learnt to walk again, we had no idea what to do with him. The psychiatrist in charge of an alcoholic unit, who has great patience with the outcasts of society, was asked to see him. He talked to the patient for some time and then sent for me. He told me that there were two possibilities; he could take him to a mental hospital under a compulsory order or he could let him go. If he took him to hospital, there was little that could be done for him except to keep him there and for Jock this would be the equivalent of a prison sentence. On the other hand, he could discharge him to the shelter in the city where he was known to the social worker, and let him go his own way. He might well drink himself to death or get knocked down again or end his life in some other way. The psychiatrist said bluntly that he might not live for more than two years if we let him go. Yet he wondered if we had any right to condemn him to what amounted to a life sentence in prison. I had no doubts as to what the answer must be. I could not shut him up for the rest of his life. He was no danger to anyone but himself and there was always the chance that in him, too, a new lease of life would enable him to live more fully than before. He went out of hospital and once or twice we had news of him, that he was seen about the city, but we will never know what happened to him. We have to be content with the thought that, as far as we could, we gave him a chance to reach out for wholeness.

All this work, which sometimes seems very tedious and concerned with the most routine details of life, raises the question whether or not it is worth it. Are we really doing good by all these hours of listening, by forming these relationships which may last only as long as the crisis persists? Is the impression that people are being made whole only an illusion? Salvation has been associated with dramatic emotional experiences for so long, that its link with wholeness has been lost sight of. It is forgotten that the goal has always been wholeness, and that the conversion experience is only the first step in a very long journey. Salvation is concerned with life and with the word of Jesus, very often not taken literally, that he came to give life in all its fullness. This is a quite simple statement that does not need to be spiritualized. It means that God intends us to live to the fullest extent of our natures, developing and using every part of ourselves. We are not saved until we have been developed to the limit of our capacity, and have achieved complete wholeness. This is a long process and few of us can claim that we have arrived. We can only press on towards the goal. If this is the end of life, then ministry has as its task the furthering of this end. The service of other people has no meaning if used for other ends, such as the filling of pews or the adding of numbers to the membership of the church. Ministry stems from a belief in the possibility of wholeness, which is rooted in faith in the Resurrection, not just as a basis for a doctrine of life after death, but as an essential force in life here and now, as new life coming to birth out of suffering and death. Ministry is the fanning into flame of this spark of life, the fostering of it, arousing faith in its existence when all seems hopeless and dead. Ministry does not necessarily need to speak of God or prove his existence. Every act, offering life and presenting the possibility of wholeness, is a witness to the living God.

10 The Casework Ministry

Many who practise casework see it as a worthwhile job and a necessary one in present-day society, but do not consider it to be in any sense a vocation. While they accept the values and principles underlying it they would not agree that it in any way implies acceptance of a particular set of religious beliefs. In *The Faith of the Counsellors*, Professor Halmos suggests that we are living in the age of post-political man. It is no longer possible in the affluent society to be interested in political issues which are concerned with society as a whole or with large sections of it. The shift of interest in social science has been to individuals and small groups and has a therapeutic rather than a political emphasis. It is in this milieu that the role of the secular counsellor has grown up and has taken over some of the former functioning of both the doctor and the priest. Post-political man is concerned with personal unhappiness in human relationships and according to this view he becomes a counsellor because he has a secret hope that by dealing with personal needs he will somehow bring in a kind of humanistic kingdom of God.[1] While some critics have objected to the statement that we live in a post-political age and that we are disillusioned with political solutions, many social workers would agree with this definition of a counsellor as one who puts his trust in salvation through personal relationships, rather than in ideologies, whether political or religious.

In *The Personal Service Society*[2] Professor Halmos goes on to suggest that we are becoming a society in which the moral leadership is that of the professional, especially those working in the personal services, whose ethos is becoming accepted as the ethos of our industrial society. He takes the economists' term 'maximization' and applies it not to income but to human culture. Man, he says, is a maximizing animal, that is to say he strives towards ideals or perfections. The professional practitioner works at maximization in three directions: mastery of the knowledge and skill required for the practise of his profession; development of concern for clients' needs that becomes an increasingly sensitive empathy and perfection of professional integrity. He believes there is evidence to suggest that the desire for money and status which underlies our industrial society is being powerfully countered by these values that are the basis of the counselling professions.

Even those who cannot share Professor Halmos' optimism about the direction in which society is travelling can find in this theory a basis for what might be called a secular vocation. It fulfils a need once answered by religious communities or the foreign mission field, and now 'professionalization is a socially accepted secular occasion to depart from the rules of common sense self-interest to which we are otherwise indoctrinated to conform'.[3] Casework therefore offers a profession to those who are dissatisfied with our competitive self-assertive society and yet who are unable to accept a specifically Christian view of life.

Other caseworkers, however, see their job as a definite expression of their Christian faith and as a way of life that can be compared with some of the conventional forms of Christian living. There is a great deal of discussion today about the spiritual life, whether there is such a thing as contemporary spirituality and if so what form it takes. Casework, practised as a ministry, can be seen to be an answer for those who are aware of their need for some form of spirituality but are unable to accept the traditional forms of it.

Teilhard de Chardin wrote: 'I dream of a new St Francis or a new St Ignatius who will bring us the new sort of

Christian life we need – one that is at the same time more involved in and more detached from the world.'[4] Orthodox Christian spirituality has on the whole been firmly on the side of detachment rather than involvement. Even a great saint like Theresa of Avila, who was an accomplished statesman and who achieved very practical results in the reform of the Carmelites, believed that detachment from the world was more important than involvement in it. The ascetic strain in Christianity which has influenced much of its thinking and living from the desert fathers onwards has a mixed origin. There are in it elements of the philosophy of duality, the belief that all matter is evil and only spirit is good. There is evidence that this was not entirely alien to Jewish thought and there are examples of world renouncers in the Bible, John the Baptist, for instance. Yet it is not easy to reconcile this with the general tenor of the Bible which insists that God created the world and moreover saw that it was good. Nor it is easy to justify, for example, Simon Stylites on his pillar with Jesus' assertion that he, unlike John the Baptist, came 'enjoying life' (J. B. Phillips' translation).

Teilhard de Chardin's detachment was from the aims and ideals that do not tend towards the fulfilment and summing up in Christ to which he believed all things are moving. He believed that this great goal, envisioned by St Paul in his letter to the Ephesians, can only be achieved as we so involve ourselves in the life of the world that we take as it were the world with us in our progress towards salvation. In his *Writings in Time of War* he asked: 'Where then shall we find at last the ideal Christian, the Christian at once new and old who will solve in his soul the problem of vital equilibrium by channelling all the life sap of the world into his effort to attain the divine Trinity.'[5] He saw man's activity in the world not as an unfortunate necessity if he was to survive but a vital part of the plan of salvation, since action allows man to be continuous with God's creative power. In *Le Milieu Divin* Teilhard de Chardin says: 'The masters of the spiritual life incessantly repeat that God wants only souls. To give those words their true value we must not forget that the human soul, however independently created our philosophy represents it as being, is inseparable in its birth and in its growth from the universe into which it is born.'[6] He maintains that creation was not finished long ago but is continuing and our work serves to complete it. With everything we do we add something to the fullness of Christ, so that man is not only engaged in making his own soul but in completing the world.

If one's spiritual life is to be in involvement, then it is necessary to ask where and with what sort of events one is to be associated. The worker-priest movement has influenced many people to think of any place of work as an important sphere of ministry by virtue of their being present in it. The idea of Presence does not imply a belief in the heresy of 'taking God' to any particular group, but rather an affirmation of the belief that God is present at every point in this life and what is needed is to discover him. Those who adhere to this school of thought may be content to work quietly and obscurely for years on dull, monotonous or back-breaking jobs, convinced that God is there and that by their very presence, silent though it may be, they are in fact not only witnessing to his activity in the world but are co-operating with it.

To many people the practice of the presence of God was a well-known phrase from Brother Lawrence's little book of that name. Now it has become known as a way of living through Michel Quoist's *Prayers of Life*. In the preface he explains that the prayers were lived before they were written and originated from a group of Christians and not just from one man's experience. The basis of the prayers are everyday experiences, the common details of a priest's life and reflections on the suffering in the world today. In one of the introductory statements he says: 'The Father has put us into the world, not to walk through it with lowered eyes, but to search for him through things, events, people. Everything must reveal God to us.'[7] There follow prayers on the telephone, green blackboards, the wire fence and the underground. The last one aptly sums up the frame of mind of the author in the last line: 'Lord, since you wish it, I shall make for heaven in the Underground.'[8] Later he has a section entitled, 'All of Life Would Become Prayer', and adds that everyday life is the raw material of prayer. These prayers are not confined to the small happenings of everyday life but grapple with the central problem of salvation. In the preface to the prayer 'Lord, why did you tell me to love', Michel Quoist suggests that he who has begun to give himself to others is saved.

This is the basis of the theology Dietrich Bonhoeffer sketched in the 'Outline for a Book' he never lived to write. He describes our experience of God as 'encounter with Jesus Christ. The experience that a transformation of all human life is given in the fact that "Jesus is there only for others" ... Our relation to God is not a "religious" relationship to the highest, most powerful, and best Being imaginable – that is not authentic transcendence – but our relation to God is a new life in "existence for others", through participation in the being of Jesus.'[9] A definition of Jesus as the man for others, which entails also our vital concern for other people, is one that illuminates the experience of casework. It enables those who practise casework to interpret what they do as a truly spiritual activity, since the life lived for others is a life based on the transcendent. Martin Buber gave many people their first introduction to the idea that God can be understood in terms of relationship. He describes our relationships as two-fold, consisting of the primary words I–Thou and I–It: 'The primary word I–Thou establishes the world of relation', for 'all real living is meeting'.[10] The suggestion that the meaning of life is encounter has deep significance for those who are engaged in trying to establish contact with other people in a helping relationship. In a postscript to the

124

second edition Martin Buber points out that our communion with God is not something which happens alongside or above the everyday: 'God's speech to men penetrates what happens in the world around us, biographical and historical, and makes it for you and me into instruction message demand.'[11] Our encounters with others are in fact our encounters with God and what he says to us will be heard in the dialogue we have with others.

Concern for others is not new in Christianity, but in spite of its firm basis in the gospels it has suffered by being labelled the 'social gospel' by those who believe their concern is only with souls. It is necessary to shake off this implied criticism and bring it firmly back where it belongs, to the very core of Christian spirituality. Mollie Batten, in a paper for the Parish and People Conference of 1967, suggests that if the spiritual life is 'a most onerous quest for meaning in living', then we should 'select and concentrate upon some activity we can do well, to the limits of our powers and then relate our search for meaning to that activity in relation to all else'.[12] This means that the caseworker does not have to try to live a divided life, desperately seeking to keep 'time for God' in a life that will certainly be very busy and full of other people's problems. It will be in the perfecting of his caseworker's skill, as he listens and speaks, makes decisions and supports, that he will be hammering out the shape of his life with God. His search for meaning, or in Buber's phrase, his ability to 'say Thou to God', as he confronts each person and each situation, will be in proportion to his attention to the job in hand and to his unflagging determination to do it to the very best of his ability.

That this experience of God is shared by many people was demonstrated by the reception given to John Robinson's book *Honest to God*.[13] His chapter on 'The Man for Others', based on Bonhoeffer's phrase, expressed what others had experienced but could not put into words. They had felt that a God who is incarnate and is addressed by a name taken from human relationships must surely be found with people as well as in a life lived in isolation from human relationships. For those brought up, as I was, on a diet of the mystics, the years before *Honest to God* had elements of disillusionment and even despair. If the saints were right then the spiritual life is impossible in this secular age where so much time, energy and attention has to be given to being in the world. Together with nostalgia for the Carmelites and Trappists a strong feeling persisted that this is not what the gospels are about and that Jesus was not a 'spoiled' monk. There must be other ways of encountering God than in the cloister, I felt, and intense concern for others, especially the sick, the poor and the unlovely, could not be a second-class Christianity, in view of the large proportion of time which Jesus spent with such people. There did not, however, seem to be a theology for this type of spirituality, and most lay Christians are chary of weaving their own homespun theology. Now theologians are grappling with the problem of spirituality in a world in which God has been described on the one hand as 'the man for others', and on the other as 'dead'.

One of the most helpful concepts in modern theology for those trying to work out the theory behind their experience is Dr Ian Ramsey's 'cosmic disclosure'. In his paper in *Spirituality for Today* he explains a cosmic disclosure as

> a situation which has come alive both subjectively and objectively, where a 'plain', 'flat' situation restricted to the data of sense experience has taken on 'depth', or, as we say, 'a new dimension'. As the situation takes on depth objectively so I, as subject, take on depth subjectively; I too come alive. When I come alive in this way and realize my subjectivity, I realize also my transcendence . . . This is no supernatural separated by a gulf from the natural, but a supernatural of fulfilment, not denial.[14]

This sense of a new dimension in a situation describes clearly what is experienced sometimes in the practice of casework, when suddenly there is some fresh element or new life in the relationship that completely alters the whole aspect of the problem. Dr Ramsey suggests that in the silence that is at the heart of every cosmic disclosure, there is a meeting between God and ourselves. He also insists that there is always a permanent element of mystery about such a disclosure which no words will ever be able to explain. This is certainly true in the casework situations, for when there is real encounter the predominant feeling is always that of awe before the mystery of a human life which no psychologist, Freudian or behaviourist can completely define, just as no philosophy or theology can find words for the strangeness of the meeting with another human being. Dr Ramsey indeed maintains that cosmic disclosures occur most characteristically in personal relations, and that situations come alive most clearly where there is shared suffering or shared love. This is precisely what the caseworker is aiming to do, to share the suffering of the other person in a caring concern. That, as Professor Halmos points out, is love, however it may be disguised under casework or psychological jargon.

If Bonhoeffer was right in suggesting that the nearest we can get to a definition of God is that he is met in a new life for others, then there is justification for using the phrase 'casework ministry'. Ministry sums up the new life for others which is the irrefutable proof of our encounter with God. Casework is one way in which this new life may be lived. It is only one among a number of possible choices, including the traditional ministry, teaching, vocations connected with healing and many others. In *Incognito*, the author speaks of himself and the world as the two faces of God. The casework training aims at beginning to develop an awareness in these two spheres, self-knowledge and knowledge of the world, other people and the society in which we live. As the caseworker learns to observe, to listen, to communicate and to assess constructively his casework experience, he may find himself continually looking on these two faces of God. In so far as he accepts this encounter and tries to grow in awareness and readiness for it, then he is indeed exercising a ministry.

NOTES

1. Paul Halmos, *The Faith of the Counsellors*, Constable 1965.
2. Paul Halmos, *The Personal Service Society*, Constable 1970.
3. *Ibid.*, p.145.
4. Quoted by E. Rideau in *Teilhard de Chardin: A Guide to his Thought*, Collins 1967.
5. *Ibid.*, p.608.
6. Teilhard de Chardin, *Le Milieu Divin*, Collins 1960, p.311.
7. Michel Quoist, *Prayers of Life*, Gill & Son 1963, p.14. Reprinted by permission of the publishers.
8. *Ibid.*, p.19.
9. Dietrich Bonhoeffer, *Letters and Papers from Prison*, enlarged edition, SCM Press 1971, p.381.
10. Martin Buber, *I and Thou*, T. & T. Clark, 2nd ed. 1959, pp. 6f.
11. *Ibid.*, p.136.
12. Eric James (ed.), *Spirituality for Today*, SCM Press 1968, p.67.
13. John A. T. Robinson, *Honest to God*, SCM Press 1963.
14. *Spirituality for Today*, pp.82f.